OTHER BOOKS BY THE AUTHOR

"Sharpening the Christian's Sword."

ROOTED AND GROUNDED

AUGUSTIN ST FORT

WESTBOW
PRESS
A DIVISION OF THOMAS NELSON

WestBow Press books may be ordered through booksellers or by contacting:

WestBow Press
A Division of Thomas Nelson
1663 Liberty Drive
Bloomington, IN 47403
www.westbowpress.com
1-(866) 928-1240

ISBN: 978-1-4497-9651-8 (sc)
ISBN: 978-1-4497-9650-1 (hc)
ISBN: 978-1-4497-9652-5 (e)

Library of Congress Control Number: 2013909430

Printed in the United States of America.

WestBow Press rev. date: 07/05/2013

INTRODUCTION

Ephesians 1:18 says, "The eyes of your understanding being enlightened that ye may know the hope of his calling, and what the riches of the glory of his inheritance in the saints."

God has made it abundantly clear in His Word that we can be enriched through the knowledge of the Word. Only then will our eyes be opened and will we understand. This knowledge gives us wisdom, which empowers us to bring down the stronghold of the enemy. Proverbs 21:22 says, "A wise man scaleth the city of the mighty and casteth down the strength of the confidence thereof."

Solomon admonishes us in Proverbs 23:12, "Apply thine heart unto instruction and thine ears to the word of knowledge." The verse serves as a reminder to apply the Word of God in our lives in order to reap the fullness of the blessings of God.

Proverbs 24:5 says, "A wise man is strong; yea, a man of knowledge increaseth strength." This strength does not refer to physical strength. It is the strength that comes with knowledge. Knowledge is power. The knowledge of the Word of God will surely empower you. You will know who you are in Christ and also know what your rights and privileges in Christ are.

Proverbs 24:14 says, "So shall the knowledge of wisdom be to your soul, if you have found it, there is a prospect, and your hope will not be cut off."

These are many Christians I know who really love the Lord. They read the Bible, but, unfortunately, they have no understanding of it. They cannot get the gist of what they are reading.

At times, Christians find themselves helpless and hopeless in their daily walk with God. The local pastor is not always near, and, in addition to being able to turn to God, a person sometimes needs a human to whom he or she can turn.

Well, this book is intended to be a guide for you, along with the Bible. It is specially written to provide readers with fundamental truths in a simple yet comprehensive manner. It may be a handy source to consult by topic as the need arises, or it may be read in its entirety. Either way, you will want to keep it close at hand.

It is hoped that this book will help you to fight the good fight of faith by equipping you to walk in victory as you encounter daily challenges. The object of this book is, therefore, to enlighten Christians so that they may be wise and constructive in their decisions.

I pray to God that this book will be of tremendous help to you.

—Augustin St Fort

ACKNOWLEDGMENTS

To God be the glory for the great things He has done. I am extremely grateful to God, who has made it possible for me to write this book. To Him do I give all the praise and glory. For it is in Him that I live and move and have all my being.

I am especially indebted to my wife, Simone, who gave me tremendous support, particularly in editing many versions of this manuscript.

I am also grateful to all my partners and supporters in the ministry who, through their prayers and encouragement, have helped make this book a reality.

DEDICATION

To my wife, Simone; my daughter, Shyian; and all of
my Christian partners and supporters in my country,
the Caribbean, and other parts of the world.

TABLE OF CONTENTS

CHAPTER 1:

COMPLETE SURRENDER

The world is confused about the concept of religion, or what is commonly known as Christianity. Rather than being clear on what God expects of us, His creations, we are busy arguing over who is or is not a Christian. The term *Christianity*, at present, is used loosely, unlike when it was conceptualized during the formation of the church. In Acts 11:26, we find these words: "And when he had found him, he brought him unto Antioch. And it came to pass, that a whole year they assembled themselves with the church, and taught much people. And the disciples were called Christians first in Antioch."

Being a Christian is more than merely belonging to a church. It is more than changing from one denomination to another. It is more than studying or understanding all doctrinal teaching in a local assembly. Christianity is not just doing good deeds or even talking about Christ. It is not having a form of godliness and yet denying the power of God (2 Timothy 3:5). It is not being a regular churchgoer or even being loyal to a local assembly.

A Christian is defined as a follower of Jesus Christ. Hence, the disciples were called by that name. These devout men were Christlike. They lived lives similar to Christ's, in both His presence and His absence. They gave up their lives solely and wholly to the teaching of Jesus Christ.

Notice that there was a change within them, as the Bible tells us in 2 Corinthians 5:17: "Therefore if any man be in Christ, he is a new creature, old things are passed away; behold, all things are become new." So why then does everybody claim to be a Christian when there is no change occurring within them? Old habits, old ways, and old attitudes are still dominating. Well, I have found a simple solution to this problem. Surrender!

The problem with most people who claim to be Christians is that they do not surrender their lives to God. You know, sometimes we make the altar call and tell the people, "Just as I am, without one *plea*." Therefore, they come just as they are and never give up. They participate in church activities and become members of the local church, but some of them simply do not understand the act of surrendering. In 1 Kings 20:24, we see a perfect example of what it means to surrender. King Benhadad asks Ahab to surrender, and he surrenders, with absolutely no reservations. This is what God means when He asks us to surrender to Him.

Be informed that to *surrender*, according to *Merriam-Webster's Dictionary*, means to "give (oneself) over to something (as an influence)." This simply means that our habits, emotions, and influence should be given to God. This should be our first step toward a victorious Christian life. We can conclude that surrendering ourselves to God is not just giving up a little habit here and there. It is not merely saying, "I surrender," during the service. It is an unrestricted act.

I want to take you on a journey through the book of Isaiah, chapter 6. We read an intriguing account of the prophet Isaiah after the death of King Uzziah. Isaiah had a vision of the holiness and sovereignty of God. In the fifth verse he says, "Woe is me"; the word *woe* indicates a curse upon a person and is the exclamation of one who is in distress or aggrieved. Isaiah saw himself inwardly. He confessed to God, "For I am undone"—which means that the work on him was unfinished. He says, "Because I am a man of unclean lips," which shows that he had not committed his lips to God. He was still allowing evil communication to proceed out of his mouth. When he says, "And I dwell in the midst of a people of unclean lips," he is saying that the people around him or those he frequently spends time with also have unclean or unsanctified lips. When Isaiah declares, "For mine eyes have seen the king, the Lord of hosts," he reveals that he is able to see the Lord in all His beauty and glory now that Isaiah's own state of unworthiness has been exposed.

What can we deduce from this verse? Well, Isaiah acknowledged who he was: "But we are all as an unclean thing, and all our righteousnesses are as filthy rags; and we all do fade as a leaf; and our iniquities, like the wind, have taken us away" (Isaiah 64:6). This, my friend, is the first step in surrendering yourself to God: acknowledge that you are a sinner and that you can't help yourself.

Let's look at verses 7 and 8: "Then flew one of the seraphim unto me, having a live coal in his hand, which he had taken with the tongs from off the altar: And he laid it upon my mouth, and said, Lo, this hath touched thy lips; and thine iniquity is taken away, and thy sin purged." Isaiah was cleansed. The placing of the coal on his lips signified his purging or purification. This is the second step. After you acknowledge your state and indicate your hopelessness, God forgives and purges you. You are transformed.

Verse 8 says, "Also, I heard the voice of the Lord, saying, Whom shall I send, and who will go for us? Then said I, Here am I; send me." Now that God has forgiven you, you are accepted by Him. Then what? Isaiah found purpose in God. The call of God was immediate. He could not keep salvation to himself alone; he also wanted to tell the world. He made himself available to God.

Complete surrendering one's life to God does not take too long. We need not make any sacrifice or penitence for God to hear and receive us. In a short space of time, Isaiah became a repented, sanctified, and purposeful man. Why? Because he made a deep surrender. That is what the church needs today—people who will surrender their very beings to Christ.

Let us now turn our attention to the apostle Paul, who is another man who lived a life surrendered to Christ. In Galatians 2:20 we find these words: "I am crucified with Christ: nevertheless I live; yet not I, but Christ liveth in me: and the life which I now live in the flesh, I live by the faith of the Son of God, who loved me and gave himself for me."

Paul is a man who completely gave himself to God. He is crucified (his old nature is gone), and yet he lives (he is a new man). The old nature is dead, but the new man is alive. He became dead to worldly habits, worldly attitudes, and fleshly desires. He wholly yielded himself to God by permitting Christ to take complete control of him. He sold out to God and thus became a slave to righteousness.

Paul reiterates in Galatians 5:24, "And they that are Christ's have crucified the flesh with the affections of lusts." The fleshly lusts must be killed or subdued. We should be following the Lord in newness of life. Again, Paul exhorts us in Ephesians 4:1, "I therefore, the prisoner of the Lord, beseech you that ye walk worthy of the vocation wherewith ye are called."

Here, Paul was admonishing believers to respect the Christian life, not only to say the name of Christ, but to live the spirit of Christianity. Jesus Christ Himself said it: "Not everyone that saith unto me, Lord, Lord, shall enter into the kingdom of heaven, but he that doeth the will of the Father which is in heaven" (Matthew 7:21).

It is not enough to call the name of God when you have not surrendered to Him. One of the reasons unbelievers do not respect the vocation wherewith we believers are called is because we speak one thing but live another. Luke 16:13 tells us, "No man can serve two masters: for either he will hate the one, and love the other; or else he will hold to one, and despise the other. Ye cannot serve God and mammon."

Let us be clear in our dealings with God: either we are on His side or we are not. We cannot be half for God and half for the Devil. God wants to own us completely. He does not want anything to stand between Him and us. In Luke 14:25–27 it says, "If any man come to me, and hate not his father, and mother, and wife, and children, and brethren, and sisters, yea, and his own life also, he cannot be my disciple. And whosoever doth not bear the cross, and come after me, cannot be my disciple."

Christ paid the price of sin, and we do not have to repay Him for His sacrifice. Neither do we have to do good works to obtain His free gift of salvation. However, God requires us to submit to Him alone and to love Him better than we love anyone else on earth. Surrendering ourselves to God also means that we have to give up everything that would separate us from Him.

Jesus knows about our love relationships here on earth. It is natural that we love our family more than anyone else. Notice the persons He makes mention of in Luke 14:25–27. In a real sense, He does not mean that we should hate these people, but He does want us to know that He is first in everything—even in our relationships. It may be difficult to give up these precious people for Christ's sake. None of them, Jesus is saying, should prevent us from fully obeying and yielding ourselves to God.

The second part of the verse is a worst-case scenario. You must hate yourself. Who does not love himself? Yet Christ says to hate yourself. You know what? Christ wants to take first place in our lives. He comes first; you and others come second. Your own will, self, lifestyle, and possessions should not be obstacles to giving yourself up to Christ. He wants your all.

Our lives should represent Jesus. He said, "Ye are the salt of the earth: but if the salt has lost his savor, wherewith shall it be salted? It is thenceforth good for nothing, but to be cast out, and to be trodden under foot of men" (Matthew 5:13). Jesus is comparing the effectiveness of a Christian to that of salt. We know that salt is important for preservation purposes. But if it becomes useless, then it is good enough to get rid of. As Christians, we need to uphold the values of Christianity. But if we are living a double standard in our Christian lives, meaning that we have not totally surrendered to Christ, then we become ineffective and thereby invite people to ridicule the gospel.

Jesus also compared the Christian to light. Matthew writes,

> Ye are the light of the world. A city that is set on a hill cannot be hid. Neither do men light a candle and put it

under a bushel, but on a candlestick; and it giveth light unto all that are in the house. Let your light so shine before men, that they may see your good works, and glorify your father which is in heaven. (Matthew 5:14–16)

How can someone give light when he has no light or when the light is dimmed? The Christian must be shining so as to give light to his household, neighborhood, community, nation—and, by extension, the world. Light gives direction; likewise, a Christian should give direction to those who are spiritually blind or lost. If Christians are the light, then they should illuminate. There was a time when we all walked in darkness, when we weren't of God (Ephesians 2:1–3), but now we are the people of God.

There is one thing I must underscore: the benefit of surrendering oneself to the Lord. As happened with the prophet Isaiah, the apostle Paul, and others who truly surrendered their lives to Christ, the experience (1) draws you nearer to God; (2) better acquaints you with God; (3) helps you to commune with God as a friend with a friend; and (4) helps you to have a better knowledge of God.

Do you want to surrender all to Jesus today? I mean your thoughts, words, deeds, home, family, business, job, music, dress, etc.? Like the song of old says, tell Jesus this:

> Have thine own way, Lord.
> Have thine own way.
> Thou art the potter,
> I am the clay.

Allow Jesus to break and mold you. Let me assure you that no one can do it for you. Also, neither sermons, nor conferences, nor workshops, nor books will do it. Only God can. Tell God, "I surrender." Only then will you experience purpose in Christ, power from on high, and total victory in your Christian walk.

Do it today!

CHAPTER 2:

MAKING CHOICES

In one of his discourses to the children of Israel, Joshua spoke to them and said,

> And if it seem evil unto you to serve the Lord, choose you this day whom ye will serve, whether the gods which your fathers served that were on the other side of the flood, or the gods of the Amorites, in whose land ye dwell: but as for me and my house, we will serve the Lord. (Joshua 24:15)

These are stupendous words coming from this man of God. Joshua wanted to show the children of Israel that they were idolaters. On the other hand, Joshua did not want them to think that he was imposing on them an obligation to serve God. He wanted them to make that choice for themselves, hence the reason he presented them with the two options, which they had to weigh. Did they want to serve the false idols that their fathers worshipped or did they want to serve the true God who brought them out of Egypt and had done so much else for them? The children of Israel had to reflect on their choice and justify their decision.

Well, Joshua informed them that he had already weighed the options and had already made his decision. Not only did he choose as an individual to serve God, but he had also made that choice for his entire household. He was quite adamant in his decision. He—and his—would serve the Lord.

In 1 Kings 18:21, a similar situation arises during the reign of the prophet Elijah.

> And Elijah came unto all the people, and said, How long halt ye between two opinions? If the Lord be God, follow him: but if Baal, then follow him. And the people answered him not a word.

From the time of creation, God has always given humankind a choice. He created people as free moral agents. God does not impose anything upon us. He has always given us the opportunity to choose. In Deuteronomy 30:19, it shows that he gave the children of Israel the choice between life and death, and between blessing and cursing.

I want you to understand that in life there is not one decision that is neutral, and so it is with serving God. As we go through our daily chores and our walk of life, we are faced with real decisions:

+ What will I be having for breakfast?
+ What menu item will I choose in the restaurant?
+ What items will I pick up in the supermarket?
+ What hairstyle will I go for in the salon?
+ What type of vehicle will I buy?
+ Which country will I visit for my holiday, and what kind of transportation will I use?
+ Which partner will I choose to marry?
+ How many children do I plan to have?

The list is inexhaustible. Notice that in all of these situations, you must make a definite decision.

Why is it so important to think of the choices that we make? Some choices carry great consequences and are not easily changed. Let us look at a possible scenario: a young girl who messes up in school and becomes pregnant outside of marriage may lose a lifetime of opportunity.

(1) She may drop out of school and never have another opportunity to complete her schooling.
(2) She may become emotionally disabled and become very vulnerable in society.
(3) Her health may be at risk.
(4) She may become dependent on her immediate family, adding more stress to a family that may already be financially burdened.

These are just some of the consequences that one bad choice may bring upon an individual.

Well, the Bible has many examples of great men and women who made choices, whether bad or good. However, the opportunity we have today is one those men and women never had. We have the privilege to read about them so that we may learn from their lives and not fall into the pit.

Let us start with Genesis 13:11, which indicates that perhaps all of us have fallen into the trap. It tells the story of God calling Abraham to leave his country, his kinsfolk, and his father's house, and then go to a land that God will lead him to. Abraham took his wife, his possessions, and Lot, his brother. Then there came a time when a choice had to be made between the two of them. Both men had great possessions, and the place where they dwelt was too small for all that they had. There was strife between their two sets of workers. Abraham called upon Lot to put an end to the strife. He gave him the opportunity to choose any part of the entire land to live on with his herdsmen and cattle. Genesis 13:11 says,

> Then Lot chose him all the plain of Jordan, and Lot journeyed east: and they separated themselves the one from another.

Who would be against himself to choose otherwise? Lot lifted up his eyes and saw that the plain of Jordan was well watered everywhere. The plain looked good and productive to Lot's eyes. Lot should have said, "Thank you, Lord, for that blessing." He didn't see a need to acknowledge God, though. Most of us would have done as Lot did. All he could see were the well-watered plains, even though they were near sinful Sodom and Gomorrah. Yet, he made a choice to stay there.

Was this a good choice? Little did Lot know that danger awaited him. The men of Sodom and Gomorrah were wicked and evil before the Lord. They were the first to commit sodomy. In fact, that's where the word *sodomy* originates from. God destroyed the two cities because they persisted in their iniquity. Our good God who promised never to destroy the righteous together with the wicked made a way of escape for Lot and his family. The decision to choose the plain of Jordan, without acknowledging God, cost Lot his wife—who turned into a pillar of salt—and all of his possessions. Lot, given the opportunity again, perhaps would not make that same choice.

What about you? You may not be in the same situation as Lot, but there are decisions that you have to make. Have you acknowledged God? Do you put Him at the center of your decisions? Or do you acknowledge Him only in difficult situations? Proverbs 3:5–6 advises us, "Trust in the Lord with all thine heart; and lean not unto thine own understanding. In all thy ways acknowledge him, and he shall direct thy paths."

Notice that these verses tell us that in all of our ways—not just in some of our ways—we should acknowledge God. Why is this so important? Because God is omniscient! Our little eyes in the natural world can only see so far, but God knows and sees everything.

In the book of Judges, chapter 14, we read of a chosen man of God who had to choose a spouse to marry. Samson, who was an Israelite, stepped out of his boundaries and asked his parents to arrange for him to marry a Philistine. Philistine was a nation against Israel at that time. His prudent parents spoke to him about the dangers and asked him to rethink the decision.

> Is there never a woman among the daughters of thy brethren, or among all my people, that thou goest to take a wife of the uncircumcised Philistines? (Judges 14:3)

Samson was adamant, like so many Christians today. "Get her for me, for she pleaseth me well." His parents knew that God was not in favor of that decision.

There are many similar situations in the church today. Oh, you really thought that Christians would take heed of Samson's downfall? Many of them become prey to the Devil. Christians pass over the church folk and go outside their Christian circle to choose a wife or husband. As they did to Samson, outsiders look pleasing to these people. They seem more attractive. They have good jobs. They have material possessions already. They have big bank accounts. And the list continues. "The young men in the church are sissies, and the young women are playing too hard to get," they think. When Christians have this mentality and view their fellow churchgoers this way, it isn't surprising that there is a high incidence of divorce among Christians.

Samson's story is a very fascinating one. Even after he lost his first wife, he continued to go the wrong way. He later married Delilah, another Philistine (Judges 16:4). Well, this time the bad choice cost him his life.

What lesson can be learned from Samson's second marriage? Sometimes God delivers us from a bad marriage despite our disobedience to Him, and then we still go the wrong way. We still choose based on what our eyes see, and we do not consult God before we make our decisions. I have seen people divorce and then remarry, still making the wrong choices. Remember, though, that God's Word is final. In 2 Corinthians 6:14–18, the Bible clearly states, "Be ye not unequally yoked together with unbelievers."

A number of reasons were identified by the apostle Paul as to why a believer should not marry an unbeliever:

(1) Deuteronomy 22:10 explains what "unequally yoked" really means. A donkey and an ox will not plow together, because one is clean and the other is unclean. Their steps are unequal and their pull is unequal. The analogy that Paul drew is that we are cleansed by the blood of Jesus, but the unbelievers are not.

(2) The Christian is righteous, which means "having good moral standards." It says in 1 John 3:7, "Little children, let no man deceive you; he that doeth righteousness is righteous, even as he is righteous." How can a righteous person have fellowship (friendly association) with the unrighteous? What communication will the two of you have? What places can interest both of you?

(3) What communion hath light with darkness? The two just cannot exist together. When light is present, there is no darkness, and vice versa. Jesus is the Light of the World. "If we say that we have fellowship with [God], and walk in darkness, we lie, and do not the truth. But if we walk in the light, as he is in the light, we have fellowship one with another, and the blood of Jesus Christ his Son cleanseth us from all sin" (1 John 1:6–7). In a nutshell, God is teaching us that only people who walk in the light and follow Him as the light should have friendly companionship.

(4) What concord has Christ with Baal? Can Christ and Satan have any agreement or harmony? No, this can never be. They have a different mission. Jesus came to give abundant life, whereas Satan comes to kill, steal, and destroy. Christ is our real Master, but Baal is an idol—and an idol is a tool of the Devil.

(5) What part hath he that believeth with an infidel? An infidel is a person who has no belief in God: an unbeliever. The person has not acknowledged the Lordship of Jesus Christ. I ask this question: What part do you, a believer, have with an unbeliever? James 3:11–12 asks, "Doth a fountain send forth at the same place sweet water and bitter water? Can the fig tree, my brethren, bear olive berries? So can no fountain both yield salt water and fresh."

We know that the answers to the given questions are "No!"; "No!"; and "No!" We must take a stand. Our choice must be clear. As a believer, do not be in a close relationship with an unbeliever.

(6) What agreement hath the temple of God with idols? What is the similarity of purpose between the temple of God and the temples that hold idols? Both are places of worship. We are the temple of the living God, as God has said: "I will dwell in them, and walk in them; and I will be their God, and they shall be my people" (2 Corinthians 6:16). As Christians, we need to give our all to God and not defile the temple of God, which is our body. Idolaters are opposed to the temple of God. We must always give God His place of worship. Be aware that great men like King Ahab, Solomon, and Samson left the true God to worship idols, which were introduced to them by foreign wives.

We should never be too close with unbelievers, so much so that they influence our decisions and actions. In Proverbs 13:20 it says, "He that walketh with wise men shall be wise: but a companion of fools shall be destroyed."

Proverbs 13:4 also states, "The law of a wise man is a fountain of life, to depart from the snares of death."

This admonition goes to you Christians who desire to have an unbeliever for a business partner—as much as possible, try to refrain from choosing that course. Your security and assurance is in Christ, while the unbelievers usually join a fraternity to get that security. The two—a believer and unbeliever—cannot work together. We cannot serve God and mammon at the same time. (Matthew 6:24)

I hope that I have not made you believe that the examples given to us in the Bible illustrate only bad choices. The Bible also has numerous accounts of people who made good choices and whom we therefore can emulate.

In Daniel 3, Shadrach, Meshach, and Abednego, three young Hebrew men, made a choice not to worship the idolatrous image that King Nebuchadnezzar had set up. The king couldn't believe what he was hearing, so he took time to explain and told them of the consequences if they refused to comply. The three men were quite assertive in their decision, despite the fiery furnace into which Nebuchadnezzar threatened to toss them. They feared God and chose to remain true to Him. Was this decision a loss for them? No. First of all, God was glorified. The king signed a decree forbidding anyone from speaking against the true and living God. Second, the three Hebrew men got a big promotion by God.

Those of us who are familiar with the account of Daniel know that he was quite loved by King Darius. Daniel was an outstanding young Jewish man who was taken into captivity by the Babylonians. He was very skilful and had an excellent spirit because the Spirit of God dwelt in him. The Babylonian men became very envious of him. They spent night and day trying to lay a trap for him. Well, of course they knew that he was a prayer intercessor, and they thought that maybe that was the only way they could get to him. They enticed King Darius to sign a decree authorizing them to throw into the lions' den anyone they found praying to God. Did that dissuade Daniel? Not at all! He did not have any secret prayer meeting. He opened his bedroom windows, knelt before God, and prayed as usual. Yes, Daniel made a choice to pray despite the consequences. Was it a bad decision? No. First of all, God was glorified. Second, his accusers were cast into the lions' den and were devoured.

We can look at many other examples of men and women who made the wisest choice. Ruth, the Moabite, made a choice to leave her people when her husband died; she followed Naomi, her mother-in-law. One of the outcomes of this choice was that the lineage of Jesus Christ came into being. Esther made a choice to go to the king when she had no right to do so. This choice led to her saving a whole nation—the Jews of Israel. Then there was Job, who made a choice to serve God throughout his calamities. He boldly said, "Though he slay me, yet will I serve him" (Job 13:15). He received a hundredfold blessing. And when Moses reached the age of forty, he made a choice between being a member of a royal family and suffering the affliction of his people. Moses chose "rather to suffer affliction with the people of God than to enjoy the pleasures of sin for a season, esteeming the reproach of Christ greater riches than the treasures in Egypt: for he had respect unto the recompense of the reward" (Hebrews 11:25–26). These are but a few examples.

Christian friends, we can never go wrong when we make a choice for God. At first, it may seem like a bad decision, but if the decision is based on the Word of God, then the blessing will follow. Hence the reason it is so important to make decisions with God as the head and at the center of each one. Always make wise decisions. For example, if you are choosing a career or a job, it is important that you ask yourself, Will the job require me to work on the days I worship? Will the job require me to stay away from doing the service of God? Will the job require me to be involved in misconduct or inappropriate behavior, or will it cause me to compromise my beliefs and values?

The choices we make today may have serious bearing on our lives tomorrow.

Now, to you who are not saved, you have an opportunity to change your choice. Well, you may wonder why I say "change your choice." Simply put, you have already made the choice not to accept Christ, hence the reason why you are on the other side of the fence. But this can be changed. In fact, this is the biggest decision that you can reverse. God wants us to make this most important choice, as this one has eternal consequences. You have to get this one right, the choice to serve God. As I mentioned earlier, God does not impose on anyone. He gives human beings a choice still, up to this present day. In John 3:15–16, it says this: "For God so loved the world, that he gave his only begotten son, that whosoever believeth in him should not perish but have everlasting life."

Eternal life is offered to everyone, but only whosoever believes will receive the gift. Jesus died for everyone, but you must believe in Him. Believing in Him actually means accepting Him as your Lord and Savior. To believe in Him means to obey his Word and surrender yourself to Him. To believe in Him means to receive Him in your heart as the Master of your life. In Romans 1:12, Paul writes, "But as many as received him, to them gave he the power to become the sons of God, even to them that believe in his name."

Believing in God means more than calling the name of Jesus. Not all who say, "Lord, Lord," shall be saved, but only those who do the will of God are saved. My dear friends, this choice is a personal one. You are the only one who can make it. I am sure you don't want to be separated from God when you die. Well, the decision to be with Him can only be made while you are alive. Romans 14:12 says, "Everyone shall give an account of himself to God." Notice that it says *everyone*. No one will stand for you. What account will you give to God? When you choose life with God, your name will be written in the Book of Life. Make a choice while you may. Revelation 20:15 says, "And whosoever was not found written in the book of life was cast into the lake of fire."

Yes, whether or not to gain eternal life is a serious choice for you to make. It is a choice between God and sex; a choice between God and alcohol; a choice between God and religion; a choice between God and pride; a choice between God and fame; a choice between God and materialism; a choice between God and the Devil.

As I close this chapter, I implore you, as Joshua did the children of Israel, choose ye this day whom you will serve. If you are serious and want to serve God, pray this prayer meaningfully.

Dear God, I acknowledge that I am a sinner in need of a Savior. I ask that You forgive me and cleanse me with the blood of Jesus. Lord, be Lord and Savior of my life. I now surrender all to You; give me the grace to walk in the light of Your Word, and may the Holy Spirit guide me from now until I end my journey on earth. In Jesus' name I pray with thanksgiving. Amen!

May God help us to make wise choices for His honor and glory.

CHAPTER 3:

THE ASSURANCE OF NOT FALLING FROM FAITH

As an evangelist, I often come into contact with many unbelievers who are well convicted by the Spirit of God after a crusade, during an open-air service, or at a church service. In the end, however, many of them do not surrender to the Lord. Regrettably, one of the main excuses that they make is that they are afraid to make a commitment, lest they fall.

In the Christian circle it is different. Everybody has made a decision to serve God, but there is still a huge problem—believers keep on falling from the grace of God. Have you ever wondered why? There are many fundamental reasons for why this is happening and recurring. Ask yourself the following questions, and see if your answers don't give you insight into why so many Christians continue to fall out of faith.

(1) Is the message that a person must maintain his or her faith delivered regularly in the church?

(2) Does the Christian know what precautionary measures to take to avoid the catastrophe of falling from grace?

(3) Does the pastor take time to counsel the believer?

(4) What other support does the church offer in this regard?

These are concerns for every believer, but they are of particular importance for pastors. God has given pastors the mandate to feed His flock, His sheep and lambs (John 21:17–17). A minister's job is to teach the people of God the doctrines of the Bible, to prepare spiritual food for everyone, no matter the state, case, or circumstance. Serve this food to the weak, the not so weak, and even the strong. Serve it personally, in small groups, and sometimes to a whole congregation.

I am very saddened by the situation in the church: many believers are constantly living in sin. Some of them have created a new doctrine to justify themselves, and their misconceptions are dangerous. Some of them use the Scripture, "For a just man falleth seven times and riseth up again" (Proverbs 24:16), as justification for their own bad behavior.

My people, do not twist the Word of God to make yourself feel good. God never intends for us to sink into sin. In 1 John 3:6–9, God makes it abundantly clear that as believers we should not continue in or practice sin. We should not live under the power and dominion of sin. If we do, then we are of the Devil.

This point is iterated in Romans 6:1–2:

> What shall we say then? Shall we continue in sin that grace may abound? God forbid. How shall we, that are dead to sin, live any longer therein?

God knows that from time to time we may violate His Word and act contrary to His command, hence He tells us, "If you sin, then you have an advocate" (1 John 2:1). But He is not pleased when we practice sin continually.

My purpose for writing this chapter is to create and heighten awareness among Christians and those intent on becoming Christians about how the Word of God has made provisions for us not to fall from the Christian faith. There are some vital principles outlined in the Word, and if we obey them, then we shall be victorious in our Christian walk.

First of all, bear in mind the scars and stains that damage our reputation for a lifetime. Let us take a case in which a couple is married but one partner is unfaithful. Let us look at some of the consequences (although God will indeed forgive when asked to).

(1) Sometimes the church disciplines or disfellowships the person who was unfaithful.
(2) The person is unable to be used in God's service for a while.
(3) Possibly, the couple separates or divorces.
(4) The family becomes unstable, especially if there are children in the family.
(5) Emotional and financial stress ensues.
(6) The community jeers and jests.

The list of consequences could go on.

Even when the individual has regained his or her stand, not many people trust him or her, especially the weaker Christians. Also, if the adultery led to divorce and the unfaithful spouse remarried, the second marriage may not work, either. In addition, the new spouse may throw former transgressions in the person's face.

Let us consider an unmarried individual who has been sexually impure while a member of the church. Some of the same consequences may occur. The person may experience more emotional stress. The person may ask him- or herself, "Will I be able to find a man [or woman] who can trust me, love me, and put this on the back burner?" and, "How effective can I be now?"

Yes, God has forgiven you, but always remember that we are human. God forgives and forgets, but a human forgives and does not forget. We are still flesh and blood. Memories of a person's indiscretions remain quite vivid in our eyes and minds.

I have noticed that the enemy uses a certain device to cause frustration among those who frequently fall from grace. The constant falling causes shame and embarrassment, so those who fall just quit trying to rise and therefore remain in their backslidden state. Proverbs

15:34 states, "Righteousness exalteth a nation: but sin is a reproach to any people."

It is very demeaning for Christians to fall from their faith so often. It brings shame not only upon the faller, but also to the family, the church, the wider Christian circle. It sends a bad message to the world: that our God is not able to keep us from falling. But we thank God that He has given us the assurance of faith. It says in Jude 1:24,

> Now unto Him who is able to *keep you from falling*, and to present you faultless before the presence of His glory with exceeding joy [emphasis mine].

I am sure that by now you have recognized that it is of paramount importance that you do not fall. Therefore, let us look at the principles laid out in the Word of God. These principles will help each of us safeguard ourselves from falling prey to the Devil. These principles are the foundation to victorious Christian living; and if they are the foundation, then we must build on them.

In Luke 6:47–48 it is noted:

> Whosoever cometh to Me, and heareth My sayings and doeth them, I will show you to whom he is like: He is like a man who built a house and dug deep and laid the foundation on a rock; and when the flood arose, the stream beat vehemently upon that house and could not shake it, for it was founded upon a rock.

In constructing a building, the foundation determines its resistance. When we look at the word *foundation*, there are three main elements that come into play:

(1) The depth
(2) The material
(3) The layout

When these three elements are up to standard, then you are guaranteed a strong foundation. Hence, it is so important to build you Christian life on the sure foundation of Jesus Christ, which is His Word. As we face the storms of life, be they financial, emotional, physical, marital, or sexual impurities, the Word of God has a way out for each one of us.

The apostle Peter, speaking from experience, admonishes us in 2 Peter 1:5–10 that we keep on adding until we get the sum. It is a step-by-step process as we build.

Step 1: Give due diligence. This simply means that you should do "hard work or show care and effort." You cannot afford to be careless in your Christian life and think that you will not fall. The Christian walk requires great effort and hard work on your part. Make sure that you are doing all in your power to obey the Word of God so that true holiness and godliness may follow you. Put up a barrier against everything that is contrary to the Word of God.

Step 2: With diligence, continue in faith. For without faith, you cannot please God (Hebrews 11:6). You do not need to add faith if you already have faith.

Step 3: Add virtue to your faith.

Step 4: Add to virtue knowledge. We must have knowledge of the Word of God. We can only get this knowledge by studying God's precious Word. Knowledge of the Word will teach us what is acceptable and unacceptable. No wonder David says, "Thy word have I hid in my heart that I might not sin against you" (Psalm 119:11).

Step 5: Add to knowledge temperance. Temperance here refers to self-control. Whatever we find to do, we must do it in moderation. This requires a high level of discipline, whether in the realm of work, food and drink, bodily exercise, or sex.

Step 6: Add to temperance patience. Patience here means perseverance. There will always be valleys in our Christian life. There will be bad times. There will be lonely nights. There will be thorns along the way. Whatever bad experiences you endure as a child of God, you cannot afford to give up. You must persevere and wait on Him.

Step 7: Add to patience godliness. Our lives as Christians must be a reflection of God. We must live a holy life. In Titus 2:12, Paul writes, "Teaching us that denying ungodliness and worldly lust, we should live soberly, righteously, and godly in this present world."

Step 8: Add to godliness brotherly kindness. We have to show love to all our brothers and sisters in the faith. We are all one in Christ. The Bible speaks so much to the subject of Christian love. Do you know that failing to practice brotherly kindness is a big downfall in our Christian walk? We usually love the brethren who love us, but frequently we do not love those who do not love us. Take a little time to read and ponder the following verses of Scripture: Matthew 5:43–47, Romans 13:8, Galatians 5:22, 1 John 4:7–8, and 1 Corinthians 13.

Step 9: Finally, add to brotherly kindness charity. God asked that we begin to show kindness and love toward our brethren, the household of faith first of all, and then to extend this love toward everybody. The Scripture above will lead you to the conclusion that to love is a commandment from God, and we have no choice but to obey if we want to honor God.

All of these virtues should be working in us at all times. What will happen next is that the equation will be balanced. The sum or the total will equal "never fall." Failure to abide in these Christian graces leads to barrenness, unfruitfulness, blindness, and forgetfulness. Only when we have done all of these things do we make our calling and election sure, making us impervious to falling out of our faith (2 Peter 1:10).

There are other biblical principles that we must adhere to and which are outlined in other Scriptures in the Bible.

(1) You should not be overly self-confident. This means that you cannot trust the flesh too much. Proverbs 28:26 says, "He that trusteth in his own heart is a fool; but whoso walketh wisely, he shall be delivered."

The apostle Paul in 1 Corinthians 10:12 writes, "Wherefore, let him that thinketh he standeth take heed lest he falls."

The above verses have one central message, and that is to take heed that we do not depend on our emotions, because they are not strong pillars. Put no confidence in the flesh, because it only knows sin.

(2) We should be aware of the weakness of our sinful human nature even when our spirit wants to serve God. Matthew 26:41 notes, "Watch and pray, that ye enter not into temptation: the spirit indeed is willing, but the flesh is weak." Paul puts it this way in Galatians 5:17: "For the flesh lusteth against the spirit, and the spirit against the flesh, and these are contrary the one to another, so that ye cannot do the things that ye would."

There is a constant battle between the flesh and the spirit, and as Christians we must be on our guard and do all in our power to win the fight in the spiritual realm. The apostle Paul cried—but not in despair—"Who shall be able to deliver me?"

(3) We must do all in our power to avoid the pathway of temptation. Shun every appearance of evil. This means that we should avoid anything that might be misconstrued as an evil intention and that we should not get involved in any unlawful act against God. Be assertive. Say to yourself, "I

will not fall to this temptation." We have the example of Jesus being tempted by the Devil. How did he overcome the temptations? He quoted and stood on the Word of God. Do the same. If the Devil tempts you to fornicate, then tell him what is written in the Word of God. "My body is the temple of the living God, and I will not defile it." He tempts you to steal? "Let them who stole steal no more." You can use the Word to shoot down any temptation.

(4) We must discern the intention of the Devil. As believers, we must remember that the enemy is on a mission. He will not rest until he accomplishes his goal. What is his goal? To take us out of the way of the Lord. Be on your guard at all times. Make no space for the Devil. Proverbs 4:16 declares, "For [the wicked and the evildoers] sleep not, except they have done mischief; and their sleep is taken away unless they cause some to fall."

(5) Do not give in to youthful lust. Flee youthful lusts (2 Timothy 1:22). Young people, this quote speaks to you, in particular. Apostle Paul gave this warning to Timothy, who was then a young minister. Paul knew that for a young person, there are lots of lust-based opportunities that present themselves. Hence the warning: anything that looks sinful or that may lead to sin, please, run away from it.

(6) Do not leave any open door for the Devil to walk in. Nor give place to the Devil (Ephesians 4:27). When you give an inch to the Devil, he takes a mile. Consequently, you must shut him out completely. He comes to steal, kill, and destroy (John 10:10).

(7) Recognize the dangers presented to us from afar. Solomon, the wisest man ever to live, gave us this advice in Proverbs

22:3: "A prudent man foreseeth the evil and hideth himself: but the simple pass on, and are punished."

As believers, we must not be ignorant concerning the devices of the Devil (2 Corinthians 2:11). You must have the eyes of the Spirit and see the trap that the enemy is setting for you. As soon as you recognize the evil, stand on your guard. Be prudent, not foolish, in your judgment. Do not let the danger take you unawares, or else you will face the penalty.

(8) Put up a fight against your own flesh (be disciplined). "So then they that are in the flesh cannot please God" (Romans 8:8). If you obey your flesh, then you are in trouble with God, because the flesh is enmity against God. No wonder Paul says that he keeps it under subjection (1 Corinthians 9:27). Do not be controlled by the desires of your flesh.

(9) Take control of your spirit (Proverbs 25:28). Solomon says, "He that hath no rule over his own spirit is like a city that is broken down, and without walls." When you do not have control over your own spirit, you become prey to the enemy, because you will fall for anything.

(10) Let the wisdom of God rule your heart (Proverbs 2:2). The entire second chapter of the book of Proverbs presents lifetime lessons about the wisdom of God, but verse 2 says, "So that thou incline thine ear unto wisdom, and apply thine heart to understanding."

The wisdom of God gives you the capacity to make good judgments. Good judgment protects us from making wrong choices.

(11) Fear the Lord. "The fear of the Lord tendeth to life: and he that hath it shall abide satisfied; he shall not be visited with evil" (Proverbs 19:23).

Your fear of the Lord is a guard on your daily walk with God. Fearing God means to revere Him and to respect Him. If you really respect Him, then you will not want to hurt Him or sin against Him.

(12) Always remember the cost of falling (2 Peter 2:20–22). I want you to take a little time to think of your life before you came to the Lord. Peter warns us that if we turn our backs on God after having been saved, then our lives will be worse than before we believed. What if we never get a second chance to make it right with God? We will suffer eternal consequences. Now, you can't afford to go to hell.

My people, I do not want you to view me as impeccable because I write on these subjects. As a minister, I try to offer counsel. For the nearly thirty years that I have been in the faith, these principles have worked for me. Proverbs 11:14 notes, "Where no counsel is, the people fall, but in a multitude of counsel there is safety."

In contrast, Proverbs 12:15 says, "The way of a fool is right in his own eyes, but he that hearkeneth unto counsel is wise."

As a minister, I cannot prevent you from falling, but I can help you take responsibility. My duty is to teach you how to keep away from falling and to point out guidelines and the plain commands from the Word of God.

My prayer for us as believers is that God will let His Word take root in our hearts and that when we have done our all, we remain standing. We do not have to fall; we can be strong and stand in the grace of God.

Satan knows how to attack us, either through our weakness or by leading us to commit presumptuous sin. No person has ever fallen because of his or her strength; a person falls because of his or her weakness.

Therefore, stand. God's strength is made perfect in our weakness.

CHAPTER 4:

HOW TO RECEIVE YOUR PHYSICAL HEALING

God has always been interested in the total human—that is, body, soul, and spirit. Although there are instances in the Bible where God has punished people for their sins (Numbers 12:1–10; Acts 12:23), generally speaking, when a child of God is inflicted with sickness, God is not unconcerned.

Frequently, sickness brings glory to God. In John 9:1–3, the disciples ask Jesus why a particular man was born blind. Jesus replies, "Neither hath this man sinned, nor his parents: but that the works of God should be made manifest in him."

I am of the belief that God wants to manifest His works even in our generation. He wants to heal us.

In this chapter, you will discover that the atonement of Jesus was not only for our sins but also for our physical healing. Our healing is equal to our forgiveness.

One should not merely read the Word of God, but one must read it to find the truth therein. This truth will enable us to receive all that God has in store for us. The Word of God makes it abundantly clear that God has given us all things pertaining to this present life. He is not reserving his blessings for the future. God's words are *yea* and *amen*. It has been established in heaven. He promises all things pertaining to life (2 Peter 1:3). Do you get it?

In Isaiah 55:11, the prophet assures us that the "word of God shall accomplish that which it pleases, and it shall prosper in the things whereto he sends it."

We have absolutely no doubt when we believe that God forgives us. We believe that He died on the cross and that He shed His precious blood for our redemption. We have confidence that His blood washes away our sins. Hence the reason why we testify with boldness, that we are saved by His blood. We can find and believe all the Scriptures pertaining to forgiveness. Well, friends, I have more good news for you. The price for all your sicknesses and sins was paid at the same time. Sickness came as a result of sin, but Jesus died for both. Long before Jesus came on the scene, the prophet Isaiah had already declared,

> Surely he hath borne our griefs and carried our sorrows: yet, we did esteem him stricken, smitten of God, and afflicted. But he was wounded for our transgressions, he was bruised for our iniquities; the chastisement of our peace was upon him; and with his stripes we are healed. (Isaiah 53:4–1)

Jesus was punished for our sins and and our sickness. Every pain, every wound, and every suffering that he endured was for our healing. You see, brethren, we have a title deed as Christians. Whatever Jesus possesses, we have a right to claim it. One of the benefits listed in this deed document is our healing. According to Acts 20:28, Jesus paid the price for our sins and thereby made possible our healing.

The concept of healing is not only found in the Old Testament, but it is also revealed in the New Testament. The apostle Peter reiterates the statements made by the prophet Isaiah when he says, "Who his own self bore our sins in his own body on the tree, that we, being dead to sins, should live unto righteousness: by whose stripes ye were healed" (1 Peter 2:24).

Peter's declaration is even more conspicuous. He made it clear that our healing is not in the future or the present, but in the past. We were healed even before we were born, before we noticed any symptom. Thank God for that provision. Our healing has been obtained. This fact is also iterated in Matthew 8:16–17: "That it might be fulfilled which was spoken by Isaiah the prophet saying, Himself took our infirmities and bore our sickness."

The Bible says 'if two shall agree on earth as touching anything that they shall ask, it shall be done for them of my Father which is in heaven. (Matthew 18:19). We have Isaiah, Peter, and Matthew concurring that the price of our healing has been paid. I hope you, too, have seen the light and by faith, benefit from His healing.

Brethren, in Romans 10:17 the Bible teaches us that "Faith cometh by hearing, and hearing the word of God."

The Word of God activates our faith, especially when we hear it over and over until it quickens us and makes our faith alive. Believe every promise from the Father, and obey his every word.

Psalm 107:20: "He sent his word and healed them and delivered them from their destruction."

Psalm 119:89: "Forever, O Lord, thy word is settled in heaven."

Proverbs 4:20–21: "My son, attend to my words, incline thine ear unto my sayings. Let them not depart from thine eyes. Keep them in the midst of thine heart. For they are life unto those that find them and health to all their flesh."

Notice in Proverbs that the writer does not say, "to those who read it" but, "to those that *find* it." Beloved, when we find that Word on healing, we should hide it in our hearts, because we have found a treasure.

Exodus 15:26: "If thou will diligently hearken to the voice of the Lord thy God and will do that which is right in his sight and will give ear to his commandments and keep all his statutes, I will put none of these diseases upon thee which I have brought upon the Egyptians, for I am the Lord that healeth thee."

CONDITIONS FOR HEALING

The conditions to receive our healing are outlined in the Word of God and are basically contained in the above verses.

(1) Listen carefully to the voice, or Word, of God. Avoid all distractions, fears, and doubts.
(2) Live right.
(3) Keep the commandments, or precepts, of God (meaning, obey Him).

Let us consider some other Scriptures.

Exodus 23:25: "And ye shall serve the Lord your God, and he shall bless thy bread and thy water: I will take away sickness from the midst of thee."

Deuteronomy 7:15: "And the Lord will take away from thee all sickness and will put none of the evil diseases of Egypt which thou knowest upon thee, but will lay them upon all them that hate you."

Jeremiah 33:6: "Behold, I will bring it health and cure, and I will cure them and will reveal unto them the abundance of peace and truth."

Ezekiel 12:25: "For I am the Lord: I will speak, and the word that I shall speak shall come to pass; it shall be no more prolonged."

Numbers 23:19: "God is not a man, that he should lie. Neither the son of man, that he should repent. Hath he said, and shall he not do it? Or hath he spoken, and shall he not make it good?"

Brethren, we have reason to rejoice, because the promises of God are *yea* and *amen*. If God says it, then He will bring it to pass. Yes, indeed, He is Jehovah Rapha, the Lord, our healer. You are a child of God, and healing is your privilege. My friend, God is not only the God of yesterday, but he is also the God of today and forever.

Let us turn our attention to the New Testament. God also laid down His principles in the New Testament in order that His people be healed. In the book of James 5:14–15 we read,

> Is any sick among you? Let him call for the elders of the church, and let them pray over him, anointing him with oil, in the name of the Lord. And the prayer of faith shall save the sick, and the Lord shall raise him up, and if he has committed sins, they shall be forgiven him.

Notice the first thing to be done when you are sick: call for the elders of the church. Second, they should anoint you with oil and pray for you. Third, the prayer of faith will heal you. Finally, if you have committed sins, you will be forgiven. It can be clearly seen that this Scripture ties spiritual and physical healing to the work of salvation.

HEALING DEPENDS ON INDIVIDUAL FAITH

Individually, we have an important role to play when it comes to our healing. We must place full confidence in the Word of God. Hebrews 10:6 states, "But without faith it is impossible to please him, for he that cometh to God must believe that he is, and that he is a rewarder of them that diligently seek him."

Mark 5:34 points out, "And he said unto her, Daughter, thy faith hath made thee whole; go in peace, and be whole of thy plague."

Nobody can put trust in God for you. It takes you, and you alone, to rely on God. Just as a young child has total faith in his parents when asked to jump from a great height, so must you place that same confidence in God. The child does not hesitate or doubt but has complete assurance that he will be safe in his parents' arms.

According to 1 John 5:14–15, "This is the confidence that we have in him, that if we ask anything according to his will, he heareth us. And if we know that he hears us, whatsoever we ask, we know that we have the petitions that we desired of him."

After you have believed in God for your healing, wait in expectation. God has healed in various ways. He does not use one method. The following Scriptures prove the point.

HEALING THROUGH THE POWER OF THE WORD

Matthew 8:16: "When the evening was come, they brought unto him many that were possessed with devils; and he cast out the spirits with his word, and healed all that were sick."

Matthew 9:6: "Then saith he to the sick of the palsy, Arise, take up thy bed, and go unto thine house."

Matthew 15:28: "'O woman, great is thy faith: be it unto thee even as thou wilt.' And her daughter was made whole from that very hour."

Luke 18:41–43: "'What wilt thou that I shall do unto thee?' And he said, 'Lord that I may receive my sight.' And Jesus said unto him, 'Receive thy sight: thy faith hath saved thee.' And immediately he received his sight, glorifying God."

There is power in the Word, for the Word is God Himself. Hebrews 4:12 says,

> For the word of God is quick and powerful, and sharper than any two-edged sword, piercing even to the dividing asunder of soul and spirit and of the joints and marrow, and is a discerner of the thoughts and intents of the heart.

HEALING THROUGH THE LAYING ON OF HANDS

Luke 4:40: "Now when the sun was setting, all they that had any sick with diverse diseases brought them unto him, and he laid his hand on every one of them, and healed them."

Mark 9:34: "And he came and took her by the hand and lifted her up, and immediately the fever left her, and she ministered unto them."

HEALING THROUGH EARTHLY MEANS

John 9:6–7: "When he had thus spoken, he spat on the ground, and made clay of the spittle, and he anointed the eyes of the blind man with the clay. And said unto him, 'Go wash in the pool of Siloam.' He went his way therefore, and washed, and came seeing."

CHRISTIANS POSSESS THIS AUTHORITY TO HEAL

Mark 16:17–18: "And these signs shall follow them that believe. In my name shall they cast out devils, they shall speak with new tongues. They shall take up serpents: and if they drink any deadly thing, it shall not hurt them; they shall lay hands on the sick, and they shall recover."

Look at this verse vis-à-vis James 5:14–15. In the account of James, the authority is given only to the elders of the church, but in contrast, Mark 16:17–18 says that every believer possesses this authority: "In my name [Jesus'], they shall lay hands on the sick, and they shall recover." If or when you are sick, find another Christian or your elders to lay hands on you and pray over you. However, if no one is available, lay your own hands upon the aching part, pray, and claim your healing.

CONFESS YOUR HEALING

It is not enough to say, "I believe that God will heal me." You must work at it until you see it come to pass. In the book of James 2:13, it states, "Yea, a man may say, Thou hast faith, and I have works; show me thy faith without thy works, and I will show thee my faith by my works."

When faith begins to take root, even though you have not seen the real manifestation, you will confess positive words.

Proverbs 10:11: "The mouth of a righteous man is a well of life: but violence covers the mouth of the wicked."

Proverbs 16:23: "The heart of the wise teacheth his mouth and addeth learning to his lips."

Proverbs 12:6: "The words of the wicked are to lie in wait for blood, but the mouth of the upright shall deliver him."

Proverbs 20:20–21: "A man's belly shall be satisfied with the fruit of his mouth, and the increase of his lips shall be filled. Death and life are in the power of the tongue, and they that love it shall eat the fruit thereof."

So you see, brethren, the words that we speak make the difference. The choice remains with you whether you want to be healed or remain sick. But I admonish you in the Lord, never allow the Devil to keep you bedridden or let you go every day with pain and suffering while you continue to ask, "Do you think that I can be healed?" Start the process today if you're sick. "The devil comes the steal, kill, and destroy" (John 10:10). We are not immune to sickness. Therefore, when it comes your way, read this chapter again and again. Underline every suggested Scripture. Search your Bible for others. Read, recite, and memorize each one of them. Ask God to increase your faith and help your unbelief. Be healed in Jesus' name.

CHAPTER 5:

SPIRITUAL INNER HEALING

Inner healing is a very unpopular topic in the church today. Satan knows how powerful this process is in bringing spiritual freedom to many lives in the body of Christ; consequently, he is trying to remove the topic from our pulpits. I trust God that as you read this chapter, you will begin to recognize its importance.

Have you ever wondered why some Christians have been in the faith for several years, sometimes serving in various area of ministry, and yet they have areas of weakness and constantly fall? This is a clear sign that these people need help. Their weaknesses are like an open wound that has never healed. Christians' propensity for downfall can also be compared to building a house without a good foundation. No matter how fast you may build the house or how much you may spend on it or how beautiful it may look, if the foundation is not strong, then the house stands in danger of collapse.

Before we think of how beautiful our house will look, we need to construct a very strong foundation. This will protect our investment. Similarly, before we get ourselves involved in any ministry, we should see to it that we are healed inwardly. Inner healing is the foundation to a victorious Christian life. A good foundation strengthens your ministry.

Jesus taught us a very important lesson about strong and weak foundations. He compared the two foundations as the former's being the work of a wise builder and the latter's being the work of a foolish builder (Matthew 7:24–27).

Jesus never taught that Christians are immune from those things that would test our foundation. These are the trials of life, which in the Bible are compared to earthly weather such as rain, flood, and wind. Jesus warned us to make it our duty to build on a strong foundation so that the trials of life would not overthrow us. It gives us great joy to know that when these threats come our way we will not fall, because our foundation is strong. Hence the reason why inner healing is so powerful and necessary in a Christian's life. I am not advocating inner healing to everyone, but let me inform you that many of us need help with our inner struggles. Sometimes people come to know the Lord and constantly fall in the same area. These people have prayed secretly for years and have even fasted to overcome the weakness, but they have had no victory. Inner healing provides the victory.

Allow me to take you through the different principles of inner healing.

THE WORK OF THE HOLY SPIRIT IN INNER HEALING

No person has the power to heal you inwardly. God has not given that power to any human being. It is the work of the Holy Spirit. No one knows you better than the Holy Spirit does. He knows how to diagnose all your weaknesses. You are ever naked before the Holy Spirit. In 1 Corinthians 2:10–11, Paul writes,

> But God hath revealed them unto us by His Spirit. For the Spirit searcheth all things, yea, the deep things of God. For what man knoweth the things of a man, save the spirit of man which is in him? Even so, no man knoweth the things of God, but the Spirit of God.

This is very important: the Spirit searches our depths. Some of our spiritual diseases are very deep. Beloved, we must be more open to the Holy Spirit than we are open to a doctor. I want you to picture yourself lying naked before a doctor who is going to examine you. Why are you so relaxed in the doctor's presence even when you're naked? You realize that there are sicknesses that you cannot see, and it's only through a doctor's examination that these can be detected.

So we should be open to the Holy Spirit. Let me assure you that if you allow Him to operate on you, He will not only perform the surgery but also bring about healing. The Holy Spirit cannot be compared to a doctor, not by any means. There are things that are impossible for a doctor to do, not matter how good he or she is in the field of medicine. But this is not the case with the Holy Spirit. If you allow Him, He will never let you die. Praise God for the Holy Spirit.

King David understood the importance of opening to the Holy Spirit. He made a very serious request to God, asking Him to search him (Psalm 138:23–24). Remember, it is the Holy Spirit who searches the heart. David asked for this because he wanted inner healing.

THE IMPORTANCE OF INNER HEALING

In order to minister to people effectively, you must first be healed of wounds, hurts, and private sin or evil habits which may dominate your life. A patient may have good intentions but may be impeded to realize his dreams because of sickness. Likewise, some Christians may want to do so much for God, but because they constantly fall prey to evil habits or other weaknesses, they cannot accomplish their dream in the body of Christ.

You may be overzealous as a Christian, and yet still you are hurting inside. But the Holy Spirit cannot use your zeal while you are still in that state. Please do not be carried away like the apostle Peter, trying to use your old nature to minister to people, thinking that you are accomplishing God's will in the ministry. You need to be healed of the old sinful nature and to put on the new nature, which is in the likeness of Christ. As it says in Colossians 3:10, "And have put on the new man which is renewed in knowledge after the image of him that created him."

The apostle Peter needed inner healing in order to minister to others. As a result, Christ told him, "But I have prayed for thee that thy faith fail not, and when thou art converted, strengthen thy brethren" (Luke 22:23).

Notice that in order for us to strengthen our brethren or, for that matter, minister to others, we must first be converted, or transformed. Inner healing is the best solution. If we are not healed, then Satan will sift us as wheat. This is why it is so important for us to do all in our power to receive inner healing before we attempt to undertake any ministry.

GOALS OF INNER HEALING

Inner healing is a process that allows the Holy Spirit to search the heart and reveal the obstacles that keep you from all that God has in store for you. (Psalm 139:23-24). It has specific goals. Here are some of them.

(1) That we be set free from the bondage of the past and become suitable for our Master's use, prepared to carry out all good works. Second Timothy 2:21 points out, "If a man therefore purge himself from these, he shall be a vessel unto honor, sanctified, and meet for the master's use, and prepared unto every good work." What are the 'these' to purge oneself from? The evil things that will hinder the process of healing, such as, fleshy lust and desires.

(2) That we serve and minister in total freedom. "Now the Lord is that Spirit, and where the spirit of God is, there is liberty" (2 Corinthians 3:17).

The Holy Spirit needs to have His own way and do all that He intends to do in your life.

(3) That we behold the full manifestation of His glory. When your inner healing takes place, it qualifies you to partake of God's glory, just as it did for Moses after he met God on Mount Sinai. "But we all, with open face beholding as in a glass the glory of the Lord, are changed in the same image from glory to glory, even as by the spirit of the Lord" (2 Corinthians 3:18).

(4) That all impediments be removed from our lives, and that we be granted access to the most holy places, because we have been cleansed and healed. "Having therefore, brethren, boldness to enter into the holiest by the blood of Jesus" (Hebrews 10:19).

(5) That a full assurance of faith be created within us and that we come to God without fear. "Let us draw near with a true heart in full assurance of faith, having our heart sprinkled from an evil conscience and our bodies washed with pure water" (Hebrews 10:19).

When your conscience is clear, it ministers to your own spirit and puts you in a rightful place with God. Inner healing also helps to remove all guilt.

GETTING READY FOR YOUR SPIRITUAL HEALING

Have you ever had the experience of undergoing surgery? Although you know it is for your healing, you still fear going through it, maybe because you anticipate excruciating pain or you are afraid you might die on the operating table. Therefore, you have mixed feelings. However, since you are aware of the importance of healing, you need to speak to yourself so as to prepare for going through with the operation. This preparation takes place in your mind. You begin to visualize your healing and what joy it will bring you once the pain is gone. You must begin to see your deliverance in the Spirit, like Paul said: our suffering on earth cannot be compared with the glory which will be revealed. The benefits of healing outweigh the pain. "And be not conformed to this world, but be ye transformed by the renewing of your mind that ye may prove what is good and acceptable and the perfect will of God" (Romans 12:2).

We are to pursue what is good and acceptable and the perfect will of God. We should not only be concerned with what makes us feel good about ourselves, but we should also know and do what makes God feel good.

HINDRANCES TO INNER HEALING

There may be lots of obstacles to inner healing, and as Christians we need to be cognizant of these. This knowledge will enable us to safeguard ourselves. Following are some examples.

Your own flesh is your first obstacle. It will try to protect its interests. "For the flesh lusteth against the spirit and the spirit against the flesh, and these are contrary the one to the other so that ye cannot do the things ye would" (Galatians 5:17).

Remember, inner healing is done by the Holy Spirit, hence the reason the flesh fights against it. The two are enemies. Therefore, each individual has a role to play in his or her inner healing by not allowing the flesh to win the fight. Paul fought very hard to bring his flesh into subjection. In 2 Corinthians 4:16 he says, "For which cause we faint not; but though our outward man [flesh] perish, yet the inward man [spirit] is renewed day by day."

The fear of what people might say is your second obstacle. Very often, Christians are conscious of the need for inner healing, but sometimes they are reluctant to *admit* that need. You know what? They are afraid of what some people might say. Consequently, they are in denial. Brethren, this cover-up will kill you. Job said, "If I covered my transgressions as Adam, by hiding mine iniquity in my bosom, did I fear a great multitude or did the contempt of families terrify me that I kept silence and went not out of the door" (Job 31:33–34)?

The tendency toward self-justification is your third obstacle. Supernatural change is the end product of inner healing. Although frequently Christians know this, the flesh does not readily accept the fact that the time to reveal hidden baggage is now. There is something natural about human beings, the way that we fail to accept responsibility for our actions. We always like to play the blame game. We definitely inherited this tendency from our forebears. Let us examine Adam's reaction when God addressed him in Genesis 3:10: "And Adam said, I heard thy voice in the garden and I was afraid because I was naked and I hid myself."

Today, rather than accepting our faults, many of us try to hide them or blame others, especially when the Holy Spirit reveals them to us through another individual. But be informed, my people, that any time God exposes us or brings those hidden things to the surface, it is because He wants to heal us from them. Therefore, instead, be thankful to God. Adam continued, "The woman whom thou gavest to be with me, she gave me of the tree, and I did eat."

Eve also joined her husband in laying blame in an effort to justify her own actions: "The serpent beguiled me and I did eat" (Genesis 3:13).

The above verses help to bring the truth to light. They teach us the reasons why Christians suffer spiritually. First of all, Adam never acknowledged his fault or took responsibility for it. He blamed the woman. His wife did likewise—she blamed the serpent. The spirit of blame is contagious. It began with Adam and Eve, and it is still alive today. There is great danger in blaming others for our own condition.

Do not allow these hindrances to stand in the way of your inner healing. Learn from Adam and Eve's mistake and stop blaming others. Be honest with yourself and realize that what people think about you should not keep you from receiving inner healing. Take responsibility and deal with the hindrances.

THE DANGER OF BLAMING OTHERS

For inner healing to work perfectly, you must acknowledge your faults. Unless you do this, you will not be healed. We must not allow the spirit of pride to control us. For example, if people know that I am a fornicator, then how will they perceive me? Because I don't want them to know the truth about me, I choose to say that I was raped and was too embarrassed to mention it. But in all honesty, I did consent to fornicate. I am lying to cover up my guilt and to maintain my reputation.

The Bible tells a fascinating story about King Saul; he, too, had the problem of not acknowledging his faults. The story begins in 1 Samuel 15:9.

> But Saul and the people spared Agag and the best of the sheep and of the oxen and of the fatlings and of the lambs and all that was good and would not utterly destroy them; but everything that was vile and refuse, that they destroyed utterly.

Although the people were involved in sparing some of the animals, which was in direct disobedience to God (God had told them not to spare anything), Saul was the king and, as such, he had the final say. Therefore, he was fully responsible for his people's actions. In verses 10 and 11 of the same chapter, God tells Samuel the prophet that He is displeased with Saul because he disobeyed His commandments. Samuel then prays all night because he recognizes the seriousness of the act committed by Saul. Samuel was not on-site, but the Spirit of God was present. In like manner, God can reveal hidden acts to his servants.

In verses 19 and 20, Samuel confronts Saul.

> Wherefore then didst thou not obey the voice of the Lord, but dist fly upon spoil and didst evil in the sight of the Lord?

> And Saul said unto Samuel, Yea, I have obeyed the voice of the Lord, and have gone the way which the Lord sent me, and have brought Agag the King of Amalek, and have utterly destroyed the Amalekites.

The first mistake that Saul made was to lie to the prophet rather than admit his error. There is a similar scenario in Acts 5. Ananias and his wife Sapphira sold a parcel of land, and when approached by the apostle Peter, they lied about the price they received for it. What was the result? Each of them died immediately! Peter was not present when they sold the land, but God revealed to him that the amount they claimed they got for it was a lie. Peter told them, "You did not lie to me but to the Holy Ghost."

Saul was not prepared to accept the blame; he passed it onto others. In Acts 15:21 he says, "But the people took of the spoil, sheep and oxen, the chief of the things which should have been utterly destroyed, to sacrifice unto the Lord thy God in Gilgal."

The second major error Saul made was in blaming the people for his own disobedience to God. Saul had pride and was therefore self-centered. He was not too bothered about God. Saul also tried to deceive the prophet of God. But in verse 22, the prophet rebukes him: "Hath the Lord as great delight in burnt offerings and sacrifices, as in obeying the voice of the Lord? Behold, to obey is better than sacrifice, and to hearken than the fat of rams."

Brethren, it does not make sense to pretend or try to hide or even blame others. Do not fight with inner conviction if you see yourself in that scenario. Don't try to be engaged in the Lord's service to cover up your faults. Please, admit, confess, and ask for help. Samuel told Saul that rebellion is like the sin of practicing witchcraft, and that stubbornness is like iniquity and idolatry.

Let us sum up the consequences of Saul's sin:

(1) God rejected him as king (1 Samuel 15:23–23).
(2) God took His spirit from him (1 Samuel 16:14).

(3) An evil spirit sent from the Lord troubled him (1 Samuel 16:14).

(4) Saul lost contact with God (1 Samuel 28:6).

(5) Saul visited the medium (witchcraft) (1 Samuel 28:7–10).

(6) Saul lost the battle (1 Samuel 31:11).

(7) Saul's sons were killed (1 Samuel 31:2).

(8) Saul killed himself (1 Samuel 31:4).

These are some of the consequences that we may face if we refuse to go God's way. The Devil will try to stop us from receiving the fullest of God's blessings by beguiling us with lies, convincing us that this is the easiest way out of our problem with God. Do not be deceived by the Devil. Learn from the lessons of Saul, Ananias and his wife, and others.

GETTING READY FOR YOUR SPIRITUAL HEALING

You must have a determination within yourself in order to receive your inner healing. You must go against all odds. You may have done shameful and embarrassing things in your life—things about which you have whispered not a word to anyone—for which you feel a load of guilt. It is time, however, to have a renewed mind. For, the apostle Paul said, "The natural man receiveth not the things of the Spirit of God, for they are foolishness unto him: neither can he know them, because they are spiritually discerned" (1 Corinthians 2:14).

Therefore, when your mind is transformed, it is no longer yours but Christ's. This new mind will instruct you in that which is good for you. Paul confirms this fact when he says, "For who that know the mind of the Lord that he may instruct him? But we have the mind of Christ" (1 Corinthians 2:16).

This new mind will control your life. It will create a hunger for your inner healing that will make even those things which are bitter in you seem sweet. "The full soul loatheth a honeycomb; but to the hungry soul, every bitter thing is sweet" (Proverbs 27:7).

There are six major steps one needs to go through in order

to receive inner healing: (1) acknowledgment; (2) counseling; (3) confession; (4) humbling oneself; (5) renunciation; and (6) prayer. These things may be unpopular, but as far as God's plan is concerned, they are the medication prescribed by the Holy Spirit of God. Below, I discuss these steps in detail. I deal with each one distinctly so that you may have a clear understanding. For, unless each step is explicit, you will not be able to put it into practice.

STEP 1: ACKNOWLEDGMENT

First, you must admit that you have a problem and declare that you are ready to accept the responsibility for it. In order to do this, you must be honest. You must face the problem, no matter how shameful or embarrassing it may be. Never try to cover it up because of your fear or shame. By doing so, you may destroy yourself, as well as others who are part of it. For an illustration, let us look at the scenario involving King David and Uriah's wife, Bathsheba. In 2 Samuel 11:4–5, it is written,

> And David sent messengers, and took her; and she came in unto him, and he lay with her; for she was purified from her uncleanness: and she returned unto her house. And the woman conceived, and sent and told David, and said, I am with child.

First of all, Bathsheba's chances of resisting the king were very slim. So David committed adultery with her, which was the first sin. He thought then that all was well. After all, he had fulfilled his lustful desire. Perhaps he may have thought, "I'll ask God to forgive me." But then came the real problem: Bathsheba was pregnant. That meant trouble. His secret sin would be made known to everybody. What to do? David took the matter into his own hands. He planned to destroy a loyal servant, Uriah, who was Bathsheba's husband. Notice that he had not acknowledged his sin but was busy seeking a way out.

David recalled Uriah from the battlefield as if he were being kindhearted. "'Report to me the progress of the war, Uriah,' David inquired. 'Now go down to thy house, and wash thy feet.' And Uriah departed out of the king's house, and there followed him a mess of meat from the king" (2 Samuel 11:8).

"But Uriah slept at the door of the king's house with all the servants of his lord, and went not down to his house" (2 Samuel 11:9).

Kind David really thought that Uriah would have welcomed the opportunity to be with his wife. No, instead he slept with the other servants. David continued planning to have Uriah sleep with his wife, Bathsheba, but Uriah did not take the bait. Now David became callous and ruthless. He plotted to kill his loyal servant. He sent him back to Joab with a sealed letter. Faithful Uriah never once thought that he was carrying his own death warrant. "Put him on the front line where the battle is the fiercest, that he may be smitten and die," the letter instructed.

So, you notice how one sin leads to many others when we do not acknowledge our wrong. I am reminded of pastors who commit adultery and, because they want to maintain their status, they never want to acknowledge their sins. It also reminds me of spouses who are unfaithful but want their transgressions to remain secret. They fail to acknowledge what they have done even when they are reproved. I am also reminded of the preacher who preaches righteousness in the pulpit but practices unrighteousness, and when reproved he prefers to leave the church rather than acknowledge his sin.

Well, David went a long way in attempting to cover up his sin, but he finally came to grips with himself. But you know what? In order for that to happen, God had to come in and say, "Enough is enough, David." He used His prophet Nathan to get David back on track.

> Wherefore hast thou despised the commandment of the Lord, to do evil in his sight? Thou hast killed Uriah the Hittite with the sword, and hast taken his wife to be thy

wife, and hast slain him with the sword of the children
of Ammon. (2 Samuel 12:9)

And David said unto Nathan, I have sinned against the
Lord. And Nathan said unto David, The Lord also hath
put away thy sin; thou shalt not die. (2 Samuel 12:13)

Brethren, when we fail to acknowledge our sin, we add to our
misery. David could have repented when he committed the first act
of adultery, but he decided to add one sin to another just to cover it
up. He couldn't run away any longer, because the words of Nathan
the prophet rang too accurate to him. Only then did he actually
acknowledge his sin. Our God is ever so merciful, though. As soon as
David accepted his responsibility, God forgave him. David experienced
God's forgiveness in such magnitude that he wrote, "Blessed is he
whose transgression is forgiven, whose sin is covered. Blessed is the
man unto whom the Lord imputeth not iniquity, and in whose spirit
there is no guile" (Psalm 32:1–2).

David learned the lesson of acknowledgment. In Psalm 32:5 he
says, "I acknowledged my sin unto thee, and mine iniquity have I
not hid. I said, 'I will confess my transgressions unto the Lord,' and
thou forgavest the iniquity of my sin." In Psalm 51:3 he writes, "For I
acknowledge my transgressions; and my sin is ever before me."

STEP 2: COUNSELING

Before a wise man engages in war, he seeks good advice, or what is
commonly known as counsel. Likewise, if we are to be successful in
the process of inner healing, then we need proper guidance.

Proverbs 20:18: "Every purpose is established by counsel: and
with good advice make war."

Our victory depends on how we understand and take heed of
wise instruction. God wants us to win the battle; that's why he made
provision in the Word to guide us.

"He taught me also, and said unto me, let thine heart retain my words; keep my commandments and live" (Proverbs 4:4).

"Hear O my son, and receive my sayings; and the years of thy life shall be many. I have taught thee in the way of wisdom; I have led thee in the right paths" (Proverbs 4:10).

"When thou goest, thy step shall not be straightened; and when thou runnest, thou shall not stumble" (Proverbs 4:10–12).

"Where no counsel is, the people fall, but in the multitude of counselors there is safety" (Proverbs 11:14).

There are two main lessons to be learned from this last verse. First, when God's people fail to take counsel, they keep on falling into the same trap—and this may lead to their total separation from the local church and from God. Second, when the people of God seek counsel, there is safety or security. For Christians, the importance of counseling must be underscored. Many people believe that when they sit with a pastor, an elder, or a counselor to speak about issues which are affecting their Christian life, they are revealing their secrets. No, my friend, you are just helping yourself out of a situation that you cannot handle by yourself. If you are open and honest, then you will be advised about how to get out of the situation. Do not conceal it.

"The way of a fool is right in his own eyes; but he that hearkeneth unto counsel is wise" (Proverbs 12:15).

"I admonish you to confess your fault one to another, and pray one for another, that you may be healed" (James 5:16). Find someone you can trust. Talk to that person about your situation. Let him or her pray for you and give you counsel until you have total victory. Yes, take a bold step. Don't be ashamed. This is your victory. Walk in it, in Jesus' name.

STEP 3: CONFESSION

The act of confession is not merely saying, "I am sorry," or "I did it." If confession was so easy, then the Bible would not dwell so much on the subject. Confession entails both acknowledging your sin and having remorse. There are two categories of confession: some confessions need to be made to God alone, while some confessions must be made to God and to a person or people.

Let us look at a few examples of the principle God laid out in His Word concerning trespassing against another person.

In Numbers 5:6–7 it says,

> Speak to the children of Israel, when a man or woman shall commit any sin that men commit, to do a trespass against the Lord, and that person be guilty. Then they shall confess their sin which they have done: and he shall recompense his trespass with the principal thereof, and add unto it the fifth part thereof, and give it unto him against whom he that trespassed.

Notice what is required in order to settle a matter when someone commits a sin against another: (1) confess the sin; (2) make a trespass offering; (3) make restitution; and (4) add a fifth part. If the wronged person died, then the payment is made to a close relative. This is necessary in order that complete healing take place in the spirit and that both individuals be granted free access to God.

In another example, Jesus met with Zacchaeus, and before Jesus even brought up the wrongs he had done to other people, he said, "Behold, Lord, the half of my goods I give to the poor, and if I have taken anything from any man by false accusation, I restore him fourfold" (Acts 19:8).

What lessons can be learned from this verse? Zacchaeus was willing to give half of his goods to the poor and to restore fourfold that of those he had taken from. When we want to be totally free, we must confess and sometimes make restitution. Consider things you have stolen; although you have confessed to God, you still feel guilty. You need to go to the individual and tell him or her that you will replace what you stole. Consider conspiracy, cheating, and borrowing things that you have not returned. If your conscience is not clear, then you need to go to the individual in question and tell him or her that you will make restitution. Paul the apostle writes, "And herein do I exercise myself to have always a conscience void of offense toward God and toward man" (Acts 24:16). Paul understood that he could not make things right with God unless he had also made things right with the people he had wronged.

James also speaks on this subject. "Confess faults one to another and pray one for another that you may be healed. The effectual fervent prayer of the righteous man availeth much" (James 5:16).

Jesus, our great teacher, sums it when he says, "Therefore, if thou bring thy gift to the altar and there remember that thy brother hath ought against thee, leave thy gift before the altar, and go thy way; first be reconciled to thy brother, and then come and offer thy gift" (Matthew 5:23).

Brethren, there are some sins that require we first go to whomsoever we offended before we approach God. We can pray about it to God for the rest of our lives, but nothing will change for us until we make things right with the person we have harmed. God has principles, and no matter who we are, we must adhere to those principles. God is concerned about our inner healing. He knows how important confession is to that process. Hence the reason he gave us clear instruction to confess and make restitution.

In light of the second category of sin, God does not require that we go to a person, since we did not hurt the person or damage the person's reputation. In these cases, we can just confess our sin to God alone. As it says in Proverbs 28:13, "He that covereth his sins shall not prosper, but who confesseth and forsaketh them shall have mercy."

You realize that God wants us not only to confess our sin but also to stop practicing it. That is why it is so important to tell someone about the areas wherein you struggle all the time. You have a weakness, and you need help to overcome it. There is no small or big sin: continual sin, big or small, is equal. The moment you find yourself committing the same sin over and over, whether it be lying, stealing, cheating, gossiping, fornicating, or remaining drunk, you need to confide in someone to counsel and pray for you.

The Bible assures us, "If we confess our sins, he is faithful and just to forgive us and to cleanse us from all unrighteousness" (1 John 3:9).

STEP 4: HUMBLING ONESELF

Make yourself of no reputation. In Philippians 2:7, the Scripture says that Jesus made Himself of no reputation and took upon Him the form of a servant, and was made in the likeness of men. Jesus lived among men, but His purpose was to serve. He lived a humbled life and never sought to live His life above anybody, regardless of status, race, or nationality.

In like manner, a Christian should make him- or herself of no reputation when it comes to inner healing. This simply means that you must empty yourself of pride and selfishness and any other thing that may stand in your way of humbling yourself before God. We must all be prepared to humble ourselves and be like clay in a potter's hands. When we keep on sinning or hurting, the vessel is spoiled, but when we are humble, we give the potter an opportunity to do as he pleases with us, the clay. As we know, God is the potter, and he wants us to be healed spiritually. Will you allow Him to work on you as He pleases?

It may not be an easy thing, but in the end it will prove to have been a rewarding exercise. God will heal you of all spiritual wounds. Do not strive with Him. Remember, as Jesus made Himself of no reputation, so must we. You don't have to protect your character when you are hurting or have sinned. Do not try to live up to people's expectations or wonder what they'll think of you. Just humble yourself before your God. Do what it takes to receive your inner healing so that your soul and spirit may be free.

Isaiah 45:9: "Woe unto him that striveth with his Maker! Let the potsherd strive with the potsherds of earth. Shall the clay say to him that fashioneth it, What makest thou? or of the work, He hath no hands?"

Isaiah 28:16: "Surely your turning of things upside down shall be esteemed as the potter's clay: for shall the work say of him that made it, He made me not, or shall the thing framed say of him that formed it, He made no understanding?"

Isaiah 55:8: "Surely the Lord's ways are not our ways; neither are His thoughts our thoughts."

Brethren, we are here on earth to bring glory to God. Jesus brought glory to His father by allowing Himself to be crucified on the cross. This was the most shameful thing that could happen to anyone. But He made Himself of no reputation. We, too, must be willing to crucify pride, shame, fear, and fleshly desires. We must join the apostle Paul in saying, "I am crucified with Christ, nevertheless I live; yet not I, but Christ who liveth in me, and the life which I now live in the flesh I live by the faith of the Son of God who loved me, and gave himself for me" (Galatians 2:21).

In John 12:24–27, Jesus uses a pattern to show us how to make ourselves of no reputation so that He may be glorified. I believe we need to pay close attention to the verses.

John 12:24: "I say unto you, except a corn of wheat fall into the ground and die, it abideth alone: but if it die, it bringeth forth much fruit."

We do not like the idea of falling to the ground. It seems humiliating. Notice, however, that the nature of the ground is not to destroy the seed but to help it bring forth fruit. Brethren, likewise, we must die to false pretense and hypocrisy. We must stop guarding our hearts in the wrong way. We should come face-to-face with the truth so that we can bear fruit.

John 12:25: "He that loveth his life shall lose it: and he that hateth his life in this world shall keep it unto life eternal."

As humans, we are all concerned about our well-being, so much so that we do not want to deal with the issues that affect our soul and spirit. Do you know that we can lose our life by trying to cover up our weaknesses? We should not compromise our own flesh by giving it what it desires.

John 12:26: "If any man serves me, let him follow me, and where I am, there shall my servant be: if any man serve me, him will my Father honor."

Jesus expects us to follow Him in all things. His position as the Son of God and Savior of the world did not stop Him from making Himself of no reputation. As we are aware, He is equal with God, and yet still He lowered himself. Money, time, status in church or society—none of these things should stand in our way of following His example. Paul, in Philippians 2:8, writes, "And being found in the fashion as a man, he humbled himself and became obedient unto death, even the death of the cross."

This verse should serve as a reminder of how we should behave if we want Jesus to be glorified in us. When we humble ourselves, we make room for God to exalt us (Luke 14:11). God exalted Jesus and gave Him a name that is above every other name. Jesus wants to heal every wound in your life. He wants to lift you up above every situation. He will make every problem bow down.

STEP 5: RENUNCIATION

Let's begin with a definition so that you will be clear. Renunciation really means to declare formally that you will no longer have anything to do with something, or that you no longer recognize something.

One of the reasons why people do not receive inner healing is because they have not understood what it means to renounce. Renunciation helps to break ties with things or persons to which you have been bound. It brings freedom and puts you in a place where you can establish a new relationship with God. It is a spiritual legality that will bring about freedom. Renunciation also helps to break covenants, agreements, and habits that may control your life. It is like writing a divorce decree to legally end a failed marriage.

The apostle Paul understood this very well. He recommended it to the church of Corinth.

> But have renounced the hidden things of dishonesty,
> not walking in craftiness nor handling the word of God
> deceitfully; but by manifestation of the truth commending
> ourselves to every man's conscience in the sight of God.
> (2 Corinthians 4:2)

Every Christian should be enlightened about this important step to inner healing. Our failure to renounce robs us of peace and victory over sins and hurts of the past. It stops us from forgiving ourselves and others. We become slaves to the past. But brethren, thank God that there is a way out—renunciation. It is a powerful and effective tool against the enemy.

In the last verse we read, Paul admonished us to renounce dishonesty and the disgraceful things that are part of us. Bear in mind what is meant by renunciation. It must be done in accordance with rules. You cannot renounce something all by yourself, just as one cannot divorce by him- or herself. There must be other players involved in order for it to be legal. You need other people to help you, because already it is too big for you to handle by yourself. Hence the reason you keep on falling or continue to live with guilt. John the apostle warns us, "And hereby we know that we are of the truth and shall assure our heart before Him, for if our heart condemns us, God is greater than our hearts and knoweth all things. Beloved, if our heart condemns us not, then have we confidence toward God" (1 John 3:19–21).

Brethren, if we are already living in a condemned state, then it does not make sense to go to God in any malicious way. If we do that, then we are just deceiving ourselves, because God knows everything. According to the apostle Luke, "And herein do I exercise myself to have always a conscience void of offense toward God and toward men" (Acts 24:16).

The apostle Paul spoke extensively on the subject of having a clear conscience: "Holding faith and a good conscience, which some having put away concerning faith have made shipwreck" (1 Timothy 1:19).

"For our rejoicing in this testimony of our conscience that is simplicity and godly sincerity, not with fleshly wisdom but by the grace of God, we have had our conversation in the world, and more abundantly to you-ward" (2 Corinthians 1:12).

"Pray for us: for we trust that we have a good conscience, in all things we will live honestly" (Hebrews 13:18).

Beloved, we must have a spirit like Moses'. He renounced and broke his legal adoption right by refusing to be called the son of Pharaoh's daughter (Hebrews 11:24). He also separated himself from the Egyptians. He forsook Egypt and began a new relationship with God and his people. That's what God desires of us. We must make an open declaration and separation. Yes, you are divorcing yourself from the habits, from the oppression, from the unfamiliar spirit, and from the sins and weight, all of which so easily best you. Are you ready?

Here is an example of a renunciation prayer that will help you.

I renounce [say the name] *in Jesus' name. I announce* [say the opposite].

For example, if you are bound by a lying spirit, you just can't speak the truth. So, your prayer of renunciation would be like this:

I renounce every lying spirit in my life. I command you, spirit of the lie, to take your leave out of my body right now, in Jesus' name, and be cast into the abyss where you belong. I announce that I will speak the truth at all times. In Jesus' name, amen!

STEP 6: PRAYER

Inasmuch as prayer plays an important role in our lives, God has established conditions for answering prayers. God is under no obligation to answer our prayers unless we meet these conditions, as laid out below.

Psalm 66:18: "If I regard iniquity in my heart, the Lord will not hear me."

Isaiah 1:15: "And when ye spread forth your hands, I will hide mine eyes from you: yea, when ye make many prayers, I will not hear: your hearts are full of blood."

Isaiah 59:1–2: "Behold, the Lord's hand is not shortened, that it cannot save; neither his ear heavy, that it cannot hear. But your iniquities have separated between you and your God, and your sins have hid his face from you, that he will not hear."

Have you ever wondered to yourself, "Why isn't my prayer answered?" Your iniquity may be the reason. If this is so, then you can turn it around. You need inner healing. We need to put the Word of God in perspective, however: first things first. There is order in everything that God is involved in, beginning with creation. Hence the reason I first explained to you the steps of inner healing. Good order will establish good relations, and good relations will lead to assurance that God will answer your prayers.

First John 3:19–22: "And hereby we know that we are of the truth, and shall assure our hearts before him, for if our heart condemns us, God is greater than our heart, and know all things. Beloved, if our heart condemns us not, then we have confidence toward God. And whatsoever we ask, we receive of him, because we keep his commandments, and do those things that are pleasing in his sight."

The condition of our heart determines our confidence in God. Our confidence determines our spiritual healing.

> This is the confidence that we have in him, that if we ask anything according to his will, he heareth us. And if we know that he hear us, whatsoever we ask, we know that we have the petition that we desired of him. God is ready to do all that you ask of him. It is all left to you now. Would you humble yourself and confess to God? (1 John 5:14–15)

> If my people, which are called by my name, shall humble themselves and pray, and seek my face, and turn from their wicked ways; then will God forgive their sin and will heal thy land. And now, mine eyes shall be opened and mine ears attentive unto the prayer that is made in this place. (1 Chronicles 7:14–15)

Notice what God requires of you:

(1) That you humble yourself
(2) That you pray
(3) That you seek His face
(4) That you turn from your wicked ways

If you do those things, then God will do these things:

(1) He will forgive you.
(2) He will heal you.
(3) He will answer your prayers.

CHAPTER 6:

MATURITY IN CHRIST

The subject of maturity in the Christian's life is one which cannot be overstated. I have seen too many Christians backslide due to immaturity. I have seen churches split or brethren join other congregations as a result of immaturity. Therefore, I urge you to read this chapter prayerfully so that you may stand as a mature soldier in the body of Christ.

First of all, let us look at what maturity is. Maturity means to grow to full development to the point where you understand the Word of God and put it into practice. Every child of God needs to reach a level of maturity in Christ in order to survive in the Christian life. The apostle Paul made it abundantly clear that maturation is a process. In 1 Corinthians 13:11 he writes, "When I was a child I spake as a child, I understood as child, I thought as a child: but when I became a man, I put away childish things."

In the above verse, Paul speaks of the categorical differences between childhood and adulthood, and ultimately he is speaking of maturity. He makes it abundantly clear that each stage is characterized by a type of behavior. One can distinguish each stage of maturity by the action displayed. The Bible clearly teaches that it is by the fruits one produces that you know that person. Paul highlighted the two behaviors. When he was a child or immature, he (a) spoke as a child; (b) understood as a child; and (c) thought as a child. In fact, he was just naïve. But when he became an adult, or was developed, he did the opposite.

There are three things that happen in the process of maturing. They are these:

(1) Growth
(2) Transformation
(3) Discipline, or self-control

Let us consider each one of these growths.

GROWTH

Growth in Christianity does not refer to size or age but to the application of knowledge provided in the Word of God. Second Peter 3:18 says, "But grow in grace and in the knowledge of our Lord and Savior, Jesus Christ. To Him be glory, both now and forever."

Proverbs 24:5 emphasizes the same point observed in second Peter: "A wise man is strong, yea, a man of knowledge increaseth strength."

You can only practice what you're knowledgeable of. You prove your level of maturity by what you practice.

Hosea 4:6 puts it this way: "My people are destroyed for lack of knowledge; because thou hast rejected knowledge, I will also reject thee, thou shall be no priest to me; seeing thou hast forgotten the law of thy God; I will also forget thy children."

We can clearly see that lack of knowledge equals immaturity in Christ. Mind you, I'm not just speaking about reading or reciting the Word; I am talking about applying it. Spiritual immaturity may be likened to the physical, mental, and emotional immaturity of an infant: because he is ignorant of danger and oblivious to cause and effect, he does things that could kill him. It is only later, when he matures, that he comes to know of cause and effect and about the physics of the world. Similarly, Christians must learn, grow, and become spiritually mature in order to avoid destroying themselves.

But how do you acquire the knowledge to grow? The apostle Paul tells you. "Study to show thyself approved unto God, a workman that needeth not be ashamed, but rightly dividing the word of truth" (2 Timothy 2:15).

Isaiah 28:9 states, "Whom shall he teach knowledge? and whom shall he make to understand doctrine? them that are weaned from the milk, and drawn from the breasts."

Brethren, God really wants us to grow. Second Peter 3:18 says, "But grow in grace, and in the knowledge of our savior Jesus Christ."

Every day we need to grow in our spiritual life in order to better know and understand God in a personal way.

TRANSFORMATION

In most cases, when things are growing, they transform into another shape, appearance, and quality. However, it is not always so in the Christian life. Our transformation begins in the mind so that the appearance and quality of our lives may be changed.

Romans 12:2: "And be not conformed to this world: but be ye transformed by the renewing of your mind that we may prove what is that good, and acceptable, and perfect will of God."

Ephesians 4:23–24: "And be renewed in the spirit of your mind. And that ye put on the new man which, after God, is created in righteousness and true holiness."

Colossians 3:10: "And put on the new man which is renewed in knowledge after the image of him that created him."

As you begin to grow in knowledge, it presses you into the mold of God so that you can be transformed into His likeness. Consequently, you will display the character of God, meaning that you will think, talk, and act like Him. According to Romans 6:13, you will yield yourself as an instrument of righteousness to God.

DISCIPLINE, OR SELF-CONTROL

Discipline is necessary in every walk of life. Discipline is an integral part of life no matter who you are. However, discipline in the Christian life is not as forthcoming as it should be, and this is one of the obvious reasons for a Christian's immaturity. Notice about Adam and Eve in the garden of Eden that they didn't have the discipline to eat only what was ordained. They were permitted to eat all of the fruits except the forbidden one—but they went ahead and ate that which was forbidden them.

The apostle Paul had to fight hard to maintain discipline. He said, "I keep under my body and bring it into subjection, lest that by any means, when I have preached to others, I myself should be a castaway" (1 Corinthians 9:27).

Paul was a saved sinner like any one of us, but he had the aptitude to discipline himself. He had the inner strength to fight against his fleshly desires. It is a battle, but with maturity, it is one we can win.

Let us draw our attention to a young Hebrew man who displayed maturity in his actions. In Genesis 39:7–8 we read,

> And it came to pass after these things that his master's wife cast her eyes upon Joseph, and she said, Lie with me. But he refused, and said unto his master's wife, Behold, my master wotteth not what is with me in the house, and he hath committed all that he hath to my hand.

How many young men who were given an opportunity to lie with this prestigious woman would not have seized it? I doubt many would refuse. But Joseph did not just think of the pleasure the experience might have brought him. Rather, he thought of the consequences of his doing wrong to his master, who had placed so much confidence in him and held him in such esteem. More important, he did not want to sin against God, whom he so loved and who had bestowed so much favor upon him. Consequently, he resorted to escape.

Maturity will help us to make the right choices, and this is the type of discipline that we need as Christians. Our mind-set needs to be, "If God says it, then I will do it."

In contrast, David, a man after God's own heart, did not exercise such maturity as Joseph did, and as a result he was not disciplined enough to turn away when he saw Bathsheba from his rooftop. Although he loved God, he did not even think of the consequences of his actions, which might be far-reaching. He committed adultery with the woman and paid a heavy price for it.

Discipline is attainable in the Christian life. The Bible teaches us how to live a victorious Christian life. It contains guidelines and commands that instruct us in how to live the Word and how to exercise discipline in our everyday walk of life.

Let us pray that God will help us to be mature in character, attitude, disposition, and discipline. May we continue to grow in grace and in the knowledge of our Lord and Savior, Jesus Christ.

* * *

HOW TO PREPARE TO BEAR THE FRUIT OF MATURITY

In order for a tree to bear fruit under normal circumstances, it needs both the rain and the sun. These two elements will help the tree grow to full maturity. Then we expect it to bear fruit. If a tree does not produce fruit, then it is considered to be worthless. In comparison, if a Christian fails to grow to maturity or fails to produce fruit, then he or she is worthless.

God, in all His wisdom, has a way of aligning our circumstances so that we are given a chance to prove whether or not we are going to produce fruit.

First Peter 4:12: "Beloved, think it not strange concerning the fiery trial which is to try you as though some strange thing happened to you."

Why do you think Peter said, "Think it not strange"? He realized that we are all leaning toward one side. We love only good things. But as Christians, we must understand that there is another side to the coin as well. In order for a battery to produce electricity, it needs both a negative and a positive pole. Likewise, we need both negative and positive experiences. The negative experiences help us absorb strength from God. These help us to grow to maturity and be fruitful.

Let us look at the experiences of Job. In his early life, he was very prosperous and happy. He was the wealthiest man in the land. But later in life, and within the course of a single day, he was faced with calamity upon calamity. His wife couldn't cope with the tragedies and advised Job to curse God and die. Job had a different spirit and knew that life would not always be a bed of roses. He produced the fruit of maturity and responded to his wife, "You speak as a foolish woman. Though he slay me, yet I will trust him." Later in his discourse Job said, "The Lord giveth and the Lord taketh away."

In 1 Peter 4:13 it says, "But rejoice, inasmuch as we are partakers of Christ's suffering, that when his glory shall be revealed, ye may be glad also with exceeding joy."

Paul further stresses the notion:

> For which cause we faint not, but though our outward man perish, yet the inward man is renewed day by day. For the light affliction, which is but for a moment, works for us a far more exceeding and eternal weight of glory. (2 Corinthians 4:16–17)

Paul underwent all kinds of suffering. He understood that for his inward man to be renewed, he had to partake of the suffering of Christ. He neither gave up nor had any intention of doing so. Rather, he was glad to be part of it.

These experiences helped him to grow immensely. He counted the outward suffering as light affliction. He looked beyond the circumstances. He did not say, "A sister lied or gossiped about me, so I'll leave." He did not say, "The people in the church dislike me, so I'll quit." He did not say, "Pastor is casting remarks at me, so I'll give up."

He was unmarried. He did not say, "The flesh can't take it any longer, so therefore I'll have to look for a partner." No! He counted all as light affliction. What a strong example of bearing the fruit of maturity.

O how I wish the church would grow into maturity and produce fruit.

Let us say, like Paul says, "While we look not at the things which are seen, but the things which are not seen, for the things which are seen are temporal, but the things which are not seen are eternal" (2 Corinthians 4:18).

Brethren, the fruit that you produce in any situation indicates your level of maturity.

CONSEQUENCES OF SPIRITUAL IMMATURITY

Immaturity is a great problem in the life of any Christian and also, by extension, in the church; therefore, every child of God should be aware of it. It is the direct opposite of maturity.

Paul the apostle challenged us to strive to reach maturity. In Ephesians 4:14 he writes, "That we henceforth be no more children, tossed to and fro, and carried about with every wind of doctrine, by the sleight of men, and cunning craftiness, whereby they lie in wait to deceive."

Let's look closely at the verse: "that we ... be no more like children." What are the characteristics of children? Well, (1) they are easily influenced; (2) they are dependent; (3) they cannot make sound decisions; (4) they are weak; and (5) they are immature. These are just a few of the many characteristics of children.

Paul compares the immature Christian to a child. But Paul is essentially saying, in the first part of the verse, "I do not want you to continue as children in the faith. Take responsibility for yourselves, grow in the knowledge of the Word, and this will enable you to become strong, rooted, and grounded in the faith. Do not allow yourself to be carried away by people's opinions or by their feelings. Also, if you are given a religious book to read, I want you to differentiate between the true Word of God and erroneous information."

Why was it so important for Paul to impress on Christians that they needed to grow in maturity? The latter part of the verse gives us the answer. The deceivers and seducers lie in wait to turn the weak ones from their faith in Jesus Christ. They wait for every opportunity to do so. They are skillful at their job.

The false teachers teach with conviction. They are certain that their teaching is the truth. Whom are they going to persuade to buy in to their claims? It is the immature Christian. Paul was so passionate about the theme of immaturity that he rebuked the Hebrew church sharply. In Hebrews 5:12–13 he says,

> For when for the time ye ought to be teachers, ye have need that one teach you again which be the first principles of the oracles of God; and are become such as have need of milk, and not of strong meat. For every one that useth milk is unskillful in the word of righteousness: for he is a babe.

The emphasis of teaching in the church is really on spiritual growth and maturity. A pastor's or Christian teacher's job is to instruct his or her people so that they become strong in the faith and pass the truth onto others who may be newer in the faith. Don't you think it absurd to be in a class where you have spent three to five years learning the alphabet, and each year new students are added to the class, so you still do not know most of the letters of the alphabet?

Paul was drawing the Hebrews' attention to the fact that they should now be teachers, but instead they still require others to teach them. And notice that the teaching Paul mentions is based on the first principles of the oracles of God. In essence, Paul was saying that the Hebrews showed no improvement. They still needed to be fed with baby bottles. How awkward it is for a ten-year-old child who is otherwise normal to be fed with a bottle. If the child is abnormal, then such a thing would be understandable. However, that's the analogy Paul was making. The immature Christian, no matter how long he has been in the faith, has not yet learned the deep things of God because "he is unskillful in the word of righteousness: for he is a babe."

The apostle James also shared some light about Christians who failed to heed the Word of God so that they may become knowledgeable and act upon it.

> Be ye doers of the word and not hearers only, deceiving your own selves. For if any be a hearer of the word and not a doer, he is like a man beholding his natural face in a glass. For he beholdeth himself and goeth his way and straightaway forgetteth what manner of man he was. (James 1:22–24)

There is a common saying: "Actions speak louder than words." But for the immature Christian, it is somewhat different: "I speak the words but do not follow through with the action." We know in life that when our words are backed by our actions, we become successful. No wonder Paul writes this to the young minister: "Ever learning and never able to come to the knowledge of the truth" (2 Timothy 3:7).

In 1 Corinthians 3:1–2, Paul reiterates the consequences of immaturity. "And I, brethren, could not speak unto you as spiritual, but as unto carnal, even as unto babes in Christ. I have fed you with milk, and not with meat: for hitherto ye were not able to bear it, neither yet now are ye able."

It is obvious that if you give solid food to a baby, he will be affected by it. As a baby grows from one stage to another, he should be nourished with the right kind of food for each stage of development.

Likewise in the spiritual realm, a new convert should be taught the basic things pertaining to salvation and then grow into the more difficult principles found in the Word of God. But Paul was not seeing the people of the church at Corinth following this order. It was high time to feed them with solid food found in the Scriptures, but they were not ready to receive it. Therefore, Paul was left with little choice but to feed them on lighter topics.

Paul realized that this level of immaturity would pose serious problems to the church, hence in verses 3 and 4 he points out, "For ye are yet carnal: for whereas there is among you envy and strife and division, are you not carnal, and walking as men? For while one saith, I am of Paul, and another, I am of Apollos, are ye not carnal?"

Have we not seen or heard it? Those of us who have been in the church a long time tend to wonder how people who have been in the church longer than we have are still envious, cantankerous, divisive, unforgiving, gossiping, backbiting, and slandering, to name just a few. Well, a long time ago, Paul had given us the answer: because those people are carnal and immature. Not only are these people unprofitable to the church, but also, in the final analysis, they may lose their souls.

Do not remain in that state and say, "That's just how I am." Get up today! Become determined to grow spiritually. Pray to God, who is ever willing to help you.

The table below highlights people's reactions to difficult situations. I have categorized them into two columns—maturity and immaturity—so that you may consult this chart and determine if your own reactions are mature or immature.

MATURITY	IMMATURITY
1 Samuel 18:5: And David went out whithersoever Saul sent him, and behaved himself wisely: and Saul set him over the men of war; and he was accepted in the sight of all the people, and also in the sight of Saul's servants.	1 Samuel 18:8: And Saul was very wroth, and the saying displeased him; and he said, "They have ascribed unto David ten thousands, and to me they have ascribed but thousands. And what can he have more but the kingdom?"
2 Samuel 24:6: And he said unto his men, "The Lord forbid that I should do this thing unto my master, the Lord's anointed, to stretch forth mine hand against him, seeing he is the anointed of the Lord."	1 Samuel 28:7: Then said Saul unto his servants, "Seek me a woman who hath a familiar spirit, that I may go to her and inquire of her." And his servants said to him, "Behold, there is a woman who hath a familiar spirit at Endor."

MATURITY	IMMATURITY
Numbers 14:9: Only rebel not ye against the Lord, neither fear ye the people of the land, for they are bread for us; their defense is departed from them and the Lord is with us, fear them not.	1 Samuel 3:10: And the Lord came and stood, and called as at other times, "Samuel, Samuel." Then Samuel answered, "Speak, for Thy servant heareth." (Note here that Samuel was a young boy and did not know it was God calling him at first.)
Exodus 18:19: Hearken now unto my voice, I will give thee counsel, and God shall be with thee, be thou for the people of God, would that thou mayest bring the causes unto God.	Genesis 37:4: And when his brethren saw that their father loved him more than all his brethren, they hated him and could not speak peaceably unto him.
Numbers 13:30: And Caleb stilled the people before Moses and said, "Let us go up at once and possess it, for we are well able to overcome it."	Numbers 13:31: But the men who went up with him said, "We are not able to go up against the people, for they are stronger than we."
Psalm 141:5: Let the righteous smite me: it shall be a kindness. And let him reprove me: it shall be as an excellent oil, which shall not break my head; for yet my prayer shall be with them in their calamities.	Numbers 12:1: And Miriam and Aaron spoke against Moses because of the Ethiopian woman whom he had married, for he had married an Ethiopian woman.
Proverbs 15:1: A soft answer turneth away wrath, but grievous words stir up anger.	Exodus 16:2–3: And the whole congregation of the children of Israel murmured against Moses and Aaron in the wilderness. And the children of Israel said unto them, "Would to God we had died by the hand of the Lord in the land of Egypt, when we sat by the fleshpots and when we ate bread to the full! For ye have brought us forth into this wilderness to kill this whole assembly with hunger."
Judges 8:1–3: And the men of Ephraim said unto him, "Why hast thou served us thus, that thou called us not when thou wentest to fight with the Midianites?" And they chided him sharply. And he said unto them, "What have I done now in comparison with you? Is not the gleaning of the grapes of Ephraim better than the vintage of Abiezer? God hath delivered into your hands the princes of Midian, Oreb, and Zeeb. And what was I able to do in comparison with you?" Then their anger was abated toward him when he had said that.	Joshua 7:21: "When I saw among the spoils a goodly Babylonian garment and two hundred shekels of silver and a wedge of gold of fifty shekels weight, then I coveted them and took them; and behold, they are hid in the earth in the midst of my tent and the silver under it."

MATURITY	IMMATURITY
Proverbs 28:23: He that rebuketh a man afterwards shall find more favor than he that flattereth with the tongue.	Judges 16:4: And it came to pass afterward, that he loved a woman in the Valley of Sorek, whose name was Delilah.
Matthew 18:26–27: The servant therefore fell down and did homage to him, saying, "Lord, have patience with me, and I will pay thee all." Then the lord of that servant was moved with compassion, and loosed him and forgave him the debt.	2 Kings 12:13: However, there were not made for the house of the Lord bowls of silver, snuffers, basins, trumpets, any vessels of gold or vessels of silver from the money that was brought into the house of the Lord.
	Proverbs 22:3: A prudent man foreseeth the evil and hideth himself, but the simple pass by and are punished.
	Proverbs 5:12: And thou sayest, "How have I hated instruction and my heart despised reproof."
	Proverbs 9:8: Reprove not a scorner, lest he hate thee; rebuke a wise man, and he will love thee.
	Matthew 18:28–30: But the same servant went out and found one of his fellow servants who owed him a hundred pence. And he laid hands on him, and took him by the throat, saying, "Pay me what thou owest." And his fellow servant fell down at his feet, and besought him, saying, "Have patience with me, and I will pay thee all." And he would not, but went and cast him into prison till he should pay the debt.

CHAPTER 7:

THE CAUSES AND CONSEQUENCES OF, AND THE CURE FOR, ANGER

Have you ever tried to explain why self-control is necessary? Have you ever found yourself facing a situation and wished you had more self-control? We would all agree, I think, that self-control is necessary. The reason for this is that the natural self is always out of control. This is truth. In fact, it is biblical. Proverbs 29:15 tells us that a child left to himself will bring shame to his mother.

The problem with self began way back in the garden of Eden, when Adam and Eve sinned by putting self on the throne instead of God and threw their lot with Satan. From that time, the human race has been out of control. However, I would like to focus on one of the ways in which self manifests when it's out of control, and this is through anger.

Anger has ruined more Christian testimony than has any other sin. People are always angry because of a number of reasons: lost loved ones, loss of health, the breakup of a marriage, loss of self-respect, underachievement, and the list goes on. However, the basic cause of anger is selfishness. When someone is angry, it is usually because someone has violated his or her rights and he or she is only interested in self. Therefore, that person will do all in his or her power in order to protect those rights.

The Bible speaks extensively on the subject of anger. But let us first look at what anger is. Anger, as we understand it, is an outburst of temper or an uncontrolled vexation. It is defined as "grouchiness, animosity, or hostility." There are other words associated with anger, although these are used more forcefully and describe anger according to the different forms it takes.

These words include the following:

+ Clamor—loud confused noise or shout, especially of people complaining angrily
+ Resentment—the feeling one has when insulted, ignored, or injured
+ Revenge—deliberate returning of affliction to someone who hurt you before
+ Wrath—great anger or rage
+ Hatred—a strong dislike for or of someone
+ Unforgiveness—failing to forgive
+ Sarcasm—bitter remarks intended to hurt the feelings of someone
+ Attack—violent attempt to hurt, overcome, or defeat someone
+ Sedition—words or action intended to make people rebel against authority
+ Criticism—fault finding
+ Intolerant—not tolerant
+ Envy—feeling of disappointment and resentment, especially at another's better fortune
+ Bickering—shooting down of opponents
+ Bitterness—an unpleasant feeling

Because anger takes many disguises, many times people do not consider themselves to be angry.

I am not suggesting by any means that anger is wrong in all cases and that nobody should ever be angry. In fact, there are instances in the Bible where people were angry; Jesus is our first example. John

2:13–16 explains how and why Jesus was angry. God was also angry in Exodus 32:10 and Deuteronomy 29:28.

Everybody, no matter how modest or docile, has had some experience with anger. Acting angrily is one way in which we express the emotion. Anger is inevitable because there will always be clashes of personality and differences of opinion. Being angry is not the issue here; rather, how to deal with it is. In the words of Aristotle, "Anybody can become angry—that is easy. But to be angry with the right person, to the right degree, at the right time, for the right purpose, and in the right way—that is not within everybody's pwer and not easy."

We have discovered thus far that anger is a natural passion and that there are sometimes legitimate reasons for a Christian to be angry. There are plausible cases of justifiable anger, such as to exhibit intolerance of an action, to clear one's name, and to warn someone. Note, however, that anger should not be used to show authority, to gratify passion, or for trivial issues. Although anger in and of itself is not sinful, we do need to pay attention to it. The cost of uncontrolled anger can be high.

THE COST OF ANGER

EMOTIONAL COST

Suppression and bitterness can make a person so emotionally upset that he is "not himself." In this state, he often makes decisions that are harmful, wasteful, or embarrassing. The emotional cost of anger prevents you from performing well in your daily duties, whether they are secular or spiritual. It prevents you from enjoying your best meal. It prevents you from sleeping soundly.

SOCIAL COST

Very simply, a chronically angry person is not pleasant to work with or even be around. You have no enjoyable relationships with family members or those who are closest to you if you are always angry. It breaks down communication. It affects sexual relations. It causes you to lose respect in the eyes of others.

PHYSICAL COST

It is difficult to separate the physical price from the financial cost, because anger brings so much stress, which in turn causes physical disorders, so that chronically angry people sometimes needlessly spend thousands of dollars on doctors and drugs to try and manage their symptoms. Prolonged anger destroys our central nervous system. Whenever our nervous system becomes tense through anger, it adversely affects one or more parts of the body. This can cause headaches, hypertension, acute stress, stroke, heart failure, and other related sicknesses. It also closes doors of opportunity for things like promotions, hirings, favors, and so forth.

SPIRITUAL COST

The highest price paid for chronic anger is in the spiritual realm. It hinders or limits the work of God in an individual's life. It keeps you from being mature in Christ. It hinders God from growing in you effectively. You cannot be a fruitful Christian because you have no self-control over anger. It hinders your prayer life. It makes you lose your reputation as a Christian. It may even be a barrier for your entry into the kingdom of God. You do not want your anger to put you on dangerous ground with God.

Since uncontrolled anger can lead us to hell, the Bible has specific guidelines to help us cope with anger. Let us examine the Bible.

Ephesians 4:26: "Be angry, and sin not; let not the sun go down upon your wrath."

One can have a just reason to be angry, as Christ did when the moneychangers were buying and selling in the temple (Matthew 21:12–14). However, there are two things we must pay attention to in those verses:

(1) Excessive anger leads to wrath.

(2) Letting the sun go down on your wrath is a bad idea.

The Bible speaks to us about both issues. Anger usually gives birth to wrath. Wrath is a stronger form of anger. It's an outburst of rage. It's a violent passion. It brings temper tantrums. Wrath normally occurs when you have been provoked. This may cause your spirit to be discomposed or bitterly resentful toward someone.

The Bible warns that if you have reached this state, do not go to bed before resolving the problem. You should calm and quiet your spirit and become reconciled with your opponent. This is so important. When you sleep it's like you are dead. You really do not know what's happening around you. Suppose you do not live to see the next day? How, then, will you appear before the Lord? In the spirit of wrath? As unforgiving? Many Christians tend to gloss over this subject. They say that it is all right to be wrathful if they have been provoked. But you can see a change in the behavior or practice of people who remain wrathful. They live in prolonged resentment. If God permits them to, after about a year or so, then they will confess that they held bitterness toward the offender. God says, "Do not let the sun go down on your wrath." Reconcile with and forgive the individual immediately. Psalm 4:4 exhorts us to examine ourselves before we fall asleep. In Ephesians 4:27 we are told, "Neither give place to the devil." Do not let the Devil take over your heart by persevering in sinful anger or in wrath. Another way to avoid giving place to the Devil is by avoiding whisperers, talebearers, and slanderers.

Consider the great words of the wisest man ever to live on earth, Solomon: "He that is soon angry dealeth foolishly" (Proverbs 14:17). You disgrace yourself by doing or saying foolish things because you give in to temptation, but when your outburst is over, you must ask your opponent for forgiveness.

Proverbs 29:11 echoes this: "A fool uttereth all his mind: but a wise man keepeth it in till afterwards."

As soon as a fool hears of a matter which angers him, he makes frivolous comments before getting to the root of things. A wise man does not operate in this manner. He will take time to think. Whatever he will say, he gives it a second thought. He will not become engaged in long discourse, but he will pause to hear each matter and answer prudently. Again, we are admonished by Solomon to hold back our anger. Proverbs 19:11: "The discretion of a man deferreth his anger, and it is his glory to pass over a transgression."

Someone who gets angry before hearing the whole matter really is a fool. The Devil has been playing this trick on us for a long time. A sister or brother comes to tell us something that someone said against us, and before we find out how and why it was said—or, for that matter, if it was even said in the first place—we quickly become exceedingly angry. The verse above asks us to use our discretion, however. We should wait and listen to the merits of the provocation before reacting. And even then, when the opponent is guilty, we are admonished to forgive him.

Anger must be controlled or managed appropriately. We are instructed by Solomon how to do this.

Proverbs 16:32: "He that is slow to anger is better than the mighty; and he that ruleth his spirit than he that taketh a city."

When one can control his anger, he is stronger than any earthly king, any prime minister, or any person who is highly esteemed. It is only when you can pacify your emotions well that you become qualified as a real conqueror, according to the Bible. Let us look at two scenarios.

Second Samuel 12:5: "David burned with anger against the man and said to Nathan, As surely as the Lord lives, the man who did this thing deserves to die."

Those of you who know the story of David and Bathsheba know how he, David, took Uriah's wife after sending him to war. She got pregnant, and in trying to cover it up, David sent Uriah to the hottest spot of the war to ensure that he died in battle. Nathan, a prophet, came to David and described the scenario anonymously, and David got so angry that he made the above statement, not knowing that Nathan was really describing David's own actions.

James 1:19–20: "Wherefore, my beloved brethren, let every man be swift to hear, slow to speak, slow to wrath. For the wrath of man worketh not the righteousness of God."

We should not allow our zeal for God to produce heated arguments that will not bring glory to Him. His cause is better served by mildness and meekness than by wrath and fury.

But look at another story, in Judges 8:1–3:

> And the men of Ephraim said unto him [Gideon], Why has thou served us thus, that thou called us not, when thou wentest to fight with the Midianites? And they did chide with him sharply. And he said unto them, What have I done now in comparison of you? Is not the gleaning of the grapes of Ephraim better than the vintage of Abiezer? God hath delivered into your hands the princes of Midian, Oreb, and Zeeb: and what was I able to do in comparison of you? Then their anger was abated toward him, when he said that.

The men quarreled with Gideon before they knew of his reasons for not calling them to battle. They did not congratulate him as a military general; instead, they were disgruntled because he passed over them in assembling his army. Gideon did not flare up at their condemnations, but instead he told them that his decision not to call them up had been directed by God. He was calm and peaceful when giving his answer. He did not answer anger with anger. He reasoned the case, and so he won—that is, the others' anger toward him abated.

Proverbs 29:22: "An angry man stirs up dissension, and a hot-tempered one commits many sins."

Proverbs 15:18: "A wrathful man stirreth up strife, but he that is slow to anger appeaseth strife."

The person who is slow to anger or is patient prevents strife and also tries to arbitrate a peace between those who have fallen out with each other.

Gideon used a soft answer to promote peace, as Proverbs 15:1 instructs: "A soft answer turneth away wrath, but grievous words stir up anger."

You have heard the adage "It takes two to make a quarrel"? When someone is really angry at you, especially a cantankerous person, what do you expect? The individual will engage in name-calling, looking for your faults, looking to defame you, and bringing up the past. This is just to humiliate you. What do you do as a Christian? Should you do the same in order to protect or defend yourself? No, Solomon teaches that we must try to reason it out, returning soft words instead of harsh ones. Plead your case even if you think that you are right. Take the wrong for the sake of peace. Take time to reason it out, step-by-step, as a person of God does.

God is so serious about the issue of anger that in Proverbs 22:24 He says, "Make no friendship with an angry man, and with a furious man thou shalt not go."

"Do not associate yourself with one who is easily angered. Bad company corrupts good character" (1 Corinthians 15:33).

Ecclesiastes 7:9 says, "Be not hasty in thy spirit to be angry, for anger setteth in the bosom of fools."

This last verse warns us about becoming angry too soon, and we should all take heed. We must not allow ourselves to get out of control and behave like fools. Wise people do not spoil their reputations by behaving foolishly; rather, they do all in their power to protect those reputations. They try not to keep anger in their bosom but rather to cast it out as quickly as possible, because, like fire, anger can destroy your life in a few seconds.

SOLUTIONS TO THE PROBLEM OF ANGER

(1) Do not condone anger.
(2) Do not make excuses when your anger gets out of control.
(3) Do not jump to conclusions.
(4) Do not pass judgment too quickly. Gather all of the facts, and

even when you have them all, ask God for the grace, wisdom, and patience to either deal with or overlook the situation.

(5) Constantly ask God for the proper attitude, and always pray against the spirit of hot or quick anger working against you.

(6) Take heed of the Word of God. Read the Word, particularly those passages related to anger, and ask God to help you keep true to it (Psalm 119:9–11).

(7) Take a deep breath and count from one to ten before you react.

(8) The next time a situation presents itself to you, ask yourself whether your response will do the following:

(a) Will it glorify God?

(b) Will it build me up in the Christian life?

(c) Will it help others, or will it cause them to stumble?

Also, can you offer a prayer of thanksgiving over the situation?

If you can honestly answer these questions, then I am certain that you will be able to recognize when your anger is getting out of control.

May the good Lord strengthen you as you work on becoming victorious over that uncontrolled monster, anger.

Pray with me.

Father, You asked that I put away anger and wrath. You said that the sun should not go down on my anger. But I have allowed, in some cases, months and years to pass while I have maintained my anger. I pray for Your forgiveness. Help me to release the people who offended me. Lord, give me self-control when someone criticizes me, lies about me, or hurts me in any way. Dear Lord, You said that Your grace is made perfect in our weakness. This has been my weak area; therefore, I ask that You grant me grace. I know that if I confess, then the spirit of anger in any form shall not rule over me again. Thank You, Lord, for the victory, in Jesus' name.

CHAPTER 8:

THE WORD

This final chapter focuses on the Word. It is my hope that you will read it carefully and discern the true meaning of—and our responsibility in light of—God's Word.

The Word of God has the answers to all of life's problems. If we apply the principles laid out in God's Word, then they will work in every situation. The Word will help you to deal with any question which may arise. It will help you decide how to act or react in any given circumstance.

Satan has different strategies to use against the people of God, but his ultimate goal is to do what he is good at—that is, to kill, steal from, and destroy the human race (John 10:10). But very few people believe that God came to give life, and that to the fullest.

The Devil does not want us to develop our full potential in God. He wants to abort our God-given ability to become who God calls us to be. He makes us feel that we are worthless and that life is meaningless; hence, so many people commit suicide. But if we would read the Word of God and realize how God cares for us no matter our status or race, then we would begin to see ourselves as precious and very valuable. Let me allow you to reflect on one Scripture that touches on this very thing. Turn your Bible to 1 Corinthians 1:26–27:

> For you see your calling, brethren, how that not many
> wise men after the flesh, not many mighty, not many
> noble, are called. But God hath chosen the foolish things
> of the world to confound the wise, and God has chosen
> the weak things of the world to confound the things
> which are not, to bring to naught things that are. That
> no flesh should glory in his presence.

Yes, my brethren, He called all sorts of people, and He made great people out of all who heeded His call. Most of them were simple people who were unknown, insignificant, and poor, and who had nothing to boast about.

He used Moses, who stammered, to bring deliverance to His people in Egypt. He used Joshua to bring His people to the Promised Land. He used Esther, who was an orphan in a strange land, to save the Jewish nation. He used Joseph to save the Israelites. He used Abraham and his wife, both at an old age, to make a blessed nation. He used little David to defeat the Philistines. He used Rahab, a prostitute, to save the spies. He can use you and make something wonderful out of you. Do not discredit yourself; the Bible has good news for you.

In the preceding chapters, we discussed topics such as healing, maturity, and making choices, among others. These topics will be of no use if we do not value or believe the Word of God. The Word is the foundation for all we need and should expect in life. But you will only discover what God has in store for you when you make the Word of God part of your life. Then, the Word will help to establish and strengthen your faith so that you believe everything that comes from the mouth of God (Matthew 4:4). The Bible says, "Faith comes by hearing, and hearing by the word of God" (Romans 10:17).

It is not enough just to hear the Word of God; we must also study it. Second Timothy 2:15 says, "Study to shew thyself approved unto God, a workman that needeth not be ashamed but rightly dividing the word of truth."

We have to love the Word of God, peruse the Word of God, and meditate on the Word of God. The psalmist David admonishes us in Psalm 1:2, "Delight in the law of the Lord and meditate on it day and night."

The same is iterated in Joshua 1:8:

> This book of the law shall not depart out of thy mouth; but thou shalt meditate therein day and night, that thou mayest observe to do accordingly to all that is written therein: for then thou shalt make thy way prosperous, and then thou shalt have good success.

The only guarantee that we have of success is to obey and ponder the Word of God. As Jeremiah 15:16 states, "When your words came, I ate them, they were my joy and my heart's delight, for I bear your name, O Lord God almighty."

The prophet ate the words. He digested them. He assimilated them and made them so integral to his being that they became a part of his body, even. To meditate on the Word of God simply means to do what the prophet did when the Word of God came to him. Meditating on the Word of God is so important that we are asked to do it both day and night, so that we may be careful to abide by everything written in it.

We have an obligation to listen to and obey the Word of God. When we love the Word of God, we are eager to wholly follow all of God's commandments. We will suffer the consequences when we disobey. In the first book of Samuel 15:1–3, God sent Samuel to anoint Saul as the first king of Israel and immediately gave him an assignment.

> Samuel also said unto Saul, The Lord sent me to anoint thee to be king over his people, over Israel: now therefore hearken thou unto the voice of the word of the Lord. Thus saith the Lord of hosts, I remember that which Amalek did to Israel, how he laid wait for him in the way, when

> he came up from Egypt. Now go and smite Amalek, and
> utterly destroy all that they have, and spare them not; but
> slay both man and woman, infant and suckling, ox and
> sheep, camel and ass.

While it is true that Saul moved when God spoke, it is also true that he did not completely obey God. In verses 10 and 11 of the same chapter, the Word of the Lord again came to Samuel, and in verse 11 God shows His displeasure about Saul's disobedience.

> Then came the word of the Lord unto Samuel saying, It
> repenteth me that I have set up Saul to be king: for he is
> turned back from following me, and hath not performed
> my commandments. And it grieved Samuel; and he cried
> unto the Lord all night.

What did God instruct Saul to do? To utterly destroy all that the Amalekites had and spare them not. What did Saul do? He spared the king and kept the best of the spoils. God had said that everything that drew breath had to die in order to solve the problem of Amalek, but Saul decided to do it his way. We should never modify the Word of God. What happened in the end? Saul was rejected as king, and no matter how many sacrifices he made, he was never reaccepted. Hence, Samuel 15:22 is so often quoted among Bible readers: "Behold, to obey is better than sacrifice, and to hearken than the fat of ram."

Many people make great sacrifices to try and please God, but they fail to obey His Word. We prove our love for Christ by obeying what we read in the Bible. When you come into contact with the Word of God, it will cut out from you what is unpleasing to the Lord. He will then graft His Word onto that place of void. That's the reason James 1:21–22 says, "But be ye doers of the word, and not hearers only, deceiving your own self."

From Genesis to Revelation, God emphasizes obedience to His Word: "If you hearken unto me," "If you obey my commandments." There is always the conjunction *if*. You choose whether you will be either obedient or disobedient. *If* you are obedient, then God will deliver as promised; *if* you are disobedient, then God promises you none of his blessings. For instance, in Isaiah 1:19, God says, "If ye be willing and obedient, ye shall eat the good of the land."

Deuteronomy 11:26–27 says, "Behold, I set before you this day a blessing and a curse. A blessing, if you obey the commandment of the Lord your God, which I command you this day."

Further, in Deuteronomy 28, God pronounces blessings upon the obedient.

You notice that there are conditions one must meet in order to obtain the blessings of the Lord. The principle condition is that of *obedience*. God's great and precious promises are designed to make us partakers of His divine nature (2 Peter 1:14). However, we must believe and obey Him. The Word of God shows us where we stand in the sight of God. No, it is not left for people to judge or condemn us. The Word of God is like a mirror unto us. It shows us our blemishes. Hebrews 4:12–13 says,

> The word of God is quick and powerful, and sharper than any two-edged sword, piercing even to the dividing asunder of soul and spirit and of the joints and marrow, and is a discerner of thoughts and intents of the heart.

I don't know how lightly you have been taking the Word of God. It is more powerful than a bullet or a missile. Those carnal weapons may only pierce flesh, but the power in the Word will separate soul and spirit, joints and marrow, and will discern the thoughts and intents of the heart. The Word of God affects the body, soul, and spirit. Hence the reason why 2 Timothy 3:16 states, "All scripture is given by the inspiration of God, and is profitable for doctrine, for reproof, for correction, for instruction in righteousness, that the man of God may be perfect, thoroughly furnished unto all good works."

Anything which is profitable, people go after, because they know that at the end of the day they will make gain. The Scripture says that the Word of God has profit in it, and those who have fully embraced and accepted the pure Word of God can truly say, Yes, there is profit in it. It has profit in these things:

(1) Doctrine: a body of teaching, e.g., salvation, sin, baptism
(2) Reproof: to bring us into conformity with the will of God
(3) Correction: to refute error; to tell us what to do instead
(4) Instruction in righteousness: to help us live a godly life

The Word of God helps us to be complete, or mature. It is the Word of God that will help us to develop our full potential in God.

There is nothing to lose when you hold onto the Word of God. O how David loved the Word of God. In Psalm 119:130 he says, "The entrance of your word giveth light."

The Word of God is luminous. The Word enlightens us. It gives us direction and guidance. It eliminates ignorance and makes us wise. In Psalm 119:105 David says, "Your word is a lamp to my feet and a light to my path."

The Word of God keeps us in check. As we walk on the path Christ has laid out for us, the Word of God helps us to avoid what is wrong and to hold onto the good patterns of behavior.

Psalm 119:103: "How sweet are thy words unto my taste! Yea, sweeter than honey to my mouth."

People who have not tasted God or His Word really believe that the Word of God is burdensome. But all of His Words are coming to pass, and not one jot of the Word shall ever fail.

In conclusion, I urge you to read, study, meditate on, and apply the Word of God to your life. As you do that, do not discount any of it. Take up your responsibility to do this, because you will someday be accountable for it. It is the gateway to eternal life. Say, like Peter and the rest of the apostles, "We ought to obey God rather than man" (Acts 5:29). We must obey the instructions in the Word, and we must refrain from doing what is forbidden. If we disregard His Word, then we disregard Him also. If you love Jesus, you should love His Word also, because John 1:14 says, "And the word was made flesh and dwelt among us." That is, Jesus *is* the Word, and if we love not the Word, then we love Him not.

Let us feed ourselves on the Word of God each day so that our spirit will be well fed and remain fresh. Claim every promise of God—that is, if you obey Him. And for those who have not begun to obey and do His will, it is not too late, but you need to start sooner rather than later.

If you need to start, just whisper prayerfully, O Lord, have mercy upon me. Forgive me for walking in disobedience to Your Word. I repent of my wrongdoing and ask You to come into my heart to rule as Savior and Lord of my life. Help me to walk in obedience to Your Word every day. In Jesus' name, amen!

About the Author

Augustin St Fort is a full-time evangelist, bringing revelations to the body of Christ and preaching the uncompromised gospel, both locally and internationally, to the lost, at any cost.

He ministers with healing and deliverance to thousands of souls.

He has ministered in Canada, the United States, the United Kingdom, France, Haiti, Venezuela, Suriname, French Guiana, Guyana, Trinidad, Barbados, Dominica, Saint Vincent, Saint Maarten, Saint Croix, Guadeloupe, Martinique, Grenada, Saint Kitts and Nevis, the Dominican Republic, and Cameroon in Africa.

He is also the founder and president of a regional organization known as Love in Action Ministries. This ministry is designed to meet the physical, mental, and spiritual needs of people through gospel preaching in different denominational churches; worldwide crusades; counseling; dancing ministries; and erecting buildings for and caring for the elderly and destitute.

Mabouya Valley
P.O. Box QSR 162
Richfond, Dennery
Saint Lucia, West Indies

Tel: (758) 453 3662; 758 487 0799
Email: augustinst.fort@gmail.com